The Didache

The Teaching of the Twelve Apostles
A Different Faith – A Different Salvation

Joseph Lumpkin

The Didache
The Teaching of the Twelve Apostles
A Different Faith – A Different Salvation

Joseph Lumpkin

Copyright © 2012 Joseph Lumpkin

Fifth Estate Publishers
2795 County Hwy 57, Blountsville, AL 35031.

Second edition 2014
Cover art by An Quigley

Printed on acid-free paper

Library of Congress Control No: 2012937150
ISBN: 9781936533251

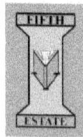

Fifth Estate

Table of Contents

Joseph Lumpkin

Didache
History and Introduction

Didache (pronounced "dih-dah-KAY" or "didah-KEY") is the Greek word meaning "teaching" or "doctrine".

The book, *"The Didache"* is also called *"The Teaching of the Twelve Apostles."* It is a treatise, consisting of sixteen short chapters. The text dates back to the earliest time of the Christian Church and was considered by some of the Church Fathers to be almost as important as the Holy Scriptures.

The Didache reveals how the Christians of the first century operated on a day-to-day basis. It is not a gospel and it does not attempt to offer a narrative the life of Jesus. In fact, some of the theology it contains runs counter to the modern interpretation of the theology in the received gospels.

The Didache represents the first concerted effort put forth by church leaders to teach the common person of the early church how to live and worship in the way the apostles of Jesus presented to their followers. This was the way of a Jewish Christian.

5

The Didache describes a path by which Gentiles and pagans could be converted, initiated, and brought into the fold to become full participants in a shared Christian life. This unity of process and teaching allowed a community, which believed itself to be poised on the threshold of the end times, to fashion its daily life in order to share the passion of the awaited return of the Kingdom of God as preached by Jesus. In fact, it is the first known instruction manual for Christian converts.

There is evidence of its use specifically by Nazarene synagogues to define and standardize the most important points of the new faith. Nazarenes were Jews who converted to a sect following Jesus. They were Hellenized Jews on the Syrian border, close to Antioch.

Certainly, the Didache was used by Jewish Christians but as Paul influenced the Nazarenes (a sect of which he was thought to be a leader), his followers diverged from the theology in the Didache. The "Pauline Christians" evolved into a separate sect leaving behind the Didache.

The Didache appears to be an "evolved" document,

meaning it has been edited, altered, or expanded over time as the early church grew and changed. There are style changes indicating the document was the creation of more than one person.

The section of the Didache titled, "There Are Two Ways," is the name of an older Jewish document and the first section of the Didache that was amended and used by several early Christian communities. This duality of presentation is also echoed in the Shepherd of Hermas and the Epistle of Barnabas. The middle two sections of the Didache may be a bit older than the first section.

The Didache was discovered in 1873 by Philotheos Bryennios, the Metropolitan of Nicomedia. It was contained in a small eleventh century codex of 120 pages. He published the text toward the end of 1883. The Didache has been the center of much academic interest and controversy since its discovery. Prior to this time its existence was known only through references by early writers. Scholars thought the text was lost to history.

Church fathers, including Athanasius, Rufinus, and John of Damascas, cited the book as inspired scripture and thus made us aware of the text. The Didache was also accepted into the Apostolic Constitutions Canon, which was written between 250-380 C.E. This compilation of eight books describes administrative canons for the clergy and the laity along with guides for worship. The books were supposed to be works of the apostles, but actually included the greater part of the *Didascalia Apostolorum,* a lost Greek treatise of 3rd century origin, along with most of the Didache, and fragments from Hippolytus and Papias. The work concludes with a collection of 85 moral and liturgical canons known as the "Apostolic Canons," a portion of which became part of canon law of the Western Church. The work is thought to be of Syrian origin. This document is also a valuable primary source on early church history and practices. It is not nearly as early a text as the Didache however.

The Didache is incorporated into a larger book which is used as part of the 81-book Ethiopic Canon. The Didache has been known in an extended Ethiopic version, called the Didascalia, which is actually part of the extended New Testament canon of the Ethiopian Orthodox Church. Many early church fathers including Barnabas, Irenaeus, Clement of Alexandria, and Origen either quote or reference the Didache.

The Didache has raised great controversy regarding its date and possible origin. Some scholars dated the text between approximately 49-79 AD. Although this is widely debated, it could place the Didache as one of the oldest Christian writings in history and date it before three of the Gospels, if not all of the Gospels.

Even though the Didache has been changed and added to over time there is strong evidence to suggest that the earliest section of it may have been penned during the time of the Jerusalem Council, around 50 AD. This would have it playing a role in the early church's controversy surrounding salvation of the Gentiles as described in the Book of Acts (ca. 50 – 100 C.E with many saying 62-64 C.E.) chapter 15.

Acts 15

New International Version (NIV)

The Council at Jerusalem

1 Certain people came down from Judea to Antioch and were teaching the believers: "Unless you are circumcised, according to the custom taught by Moses, you cannot be saved." 2 This brought Paul and Barnabas into sharp dispute and debate with them. So Paul and Barnabas were appointed, along with some other believers, to go up to Jerusalem to see the apostles and elders about this question. 3 The church sent them on their way, and as they traveled through Phoenicia and Samaria, they told how the Gentiles had been converted. This news made all the believers very glad. 4 When they came to Jerusalem, they were welcomed by the church and the apostles and elders, to whom they reported everything God had done through them. 5 Then some of the believers who belonged to the party of the Pharisees stood up and said, "The Gentiles must be circumcised and required to keep the law of Moses." 6 The apostles and elders met to consider this question. 7 After much discussion, Peter got up and addressed them: "Brothers, you know that some time ago God made a choice among you that the Gentiles might hear from my lips the message of the gospel and believe. 8 God, who knows the heart, showed that he accepted them by giving the Holy Spirit to them, just as he did to us. 9 He did not discriminate between us and them, for he purified their hearts by faith. 10 Now then, why do you try to test God by putting on the necks of Gentiles a yoke that neither we nor our ancestors have been able to bear? 11 No! We believe it is through the grace of our Lord Jesus that we are saved, just as they are."

12 The whole assembly became silent as they listened to Barnabas and Paul telling about the signs and wonders God had done among the Gentiles through them. 13 When they finished, James spoke up. "Brothers," he said, "listen to me. 14 Simon has described to us how God first intervened to choose a people for his name from the Gentiles. 15 The words of the prophets are in agreement with this, as it is written: 16 " 'After this I will return and rebuild David's fallen tent. Its ruins I will rebuild, and I will restore it, 17 that the rest of mankind may seek the Lord, even all the Gentiles who bear my name, says the Lord, who does these things'— 18 things known from long ago. 19 "It is my judgment, therefore, that we should not make it difficult for the Gentiles who are turning to God. 20 Instead we should write to them, telling them to abstain from food polluted by idols, from sexual immorality, from the meat of strangled animals and from blood. 21 For the law of Moses has been preached in every city from the earliest times and is read in the synagogues on every Sabbath." 22 Then the apostles and elders, with the whole church, decided to choose some of their own men and send them to Antioch with Paul and Barnabas. They chose Judas (called Barsabbas) and Silas, men who were leaders among the believers. **23** *With them they sent the following letter: The apostles and elders, your brothers, To the Gentile believers in Antioch, Syria and Cilicia: Greetings.* **24** *We have heard that some went out from us without our authorization and disturbed you, troubling your minds by what they said.* **25** *So we all agreed to choose some men and send them to you with our dear friends Barnabas and Paul—* **26** *men who have risked their lives for the name of our Lord Jesus Christ.* **27** *Therefore we are sending Judas and Silas to confirm by word of mouth what we are writing.* **28** *It seemed good to the Holy Spirit and to us not to burden you with anything beyond the following requirements:* **29** *You are to abstain from food sacrificed to idols, from blood, from the meat of strangled animals and from sexual immorality. You will do well to avoid these things.*

Farewell. **30** *So the men were sent off and went down to Antioch, where they gathered the church together and delivered the letter.* **31** *The people read it and were glad for its encouraging message.* **32** *Judas and Silas, who themselves were prophets, said much to encourage and strengthen the believers.* **33** *After spending some time there, they were sent off by the believers with the blessing of peace to return to those who had sent them.* **34- 35** *But Paul and*

Barnabas remained in Antioch, where they and many others taught and preached the word of the Lord.

Here, in the book of Acts, the apostles began to set a pattern that only a small list of laws needed to be kept, but the law as a whole was put aside. He question of how much Old Testament law needed to be fulfilled became a point of contention. The dispute shows up in the New testament. (The Pharisees mentioned in Act 5 were Christians.)

For the discussion within Acts to take place it must be before 64 C.E. Margherita Guarducci, who led the research leading to the rediscovery of Peter's tomb in its last stages (1963–1968), concludes Peter died on 13 October AD 64 during the festivities on the occasion of the "dies imperii" of Emperor Nero. This took place three months after the disastrous fire that destroyed Rome for which the emperor blamed the Christians. This "dies imperii" (regnal day anniversary) was an important one, exactly ten years after Nero ascended to the throne, and it was accompanied by much bloodshed.

Traditionally, Roman authorities sentenced Peter to death by crucifixion. According to the apocryphal Acts of Peter, he was crucified head down, thinking himself unworthy to die as Jesus Died. Tradition also locates his burial place where the Basilica of Saint Peter was later built, directly beneath the Basilica's high altar.

Clement of Rome, in his Letter to the Corinthians (Chapter 5), written c. 80–98, speaks of Peter's martyrdom in the following terms: "Let us take the noble examples of our own generation. Through jealousy and envy the greatest and most just pillars of the Church were persecuted, and came even unto death... Peter, through unjust envy, endured not one or two but many labors, and at last, having delivered his testimony, departed unto the place of glory due to him."

In Rome, Christians were being hunted down. Soon, in Jerusalem, Jews would be killed by the hundreds of thousands. James was killed between 62 and 69 C.E. Yet, it is my contention that Jewish Christians were targeted with greater accuracy, given the ease of recognizing them in Synagogues. Gentile Christians could hide amongst the Roman population.

To place things in perspective, here are the range of dates that encompass the writing of the earliest gospels. These are the currently accepted dates, with the earliest dates set by the more conservative religious scholars to the latest dates set by more liberal or secular scholars:

Matthew: 45 to 100 C.E.

Mark: 40 to 73 C.E.

Luke: 50 to 100 C.E.

John: 65 to 100 C.E.

Dates can be based on the events recounted in the gospels themselves. The mention of the destruction of the Jerusalem temple, which occurred in 70 C.E. could be used as a point of reference showing the text could not have been written before the event.

According to this scholarship, the gospels must have been written after the devastation because they refer to it. Conservative believers maintain the early dates demonstrate Jesus' divine powers of prophecy. They believe the Gospels were written earlier.

The Didache may have been written before Matthew, and certainly before Acts (62 – 100 C.E.). When one looks at the discussion between the apostles regarding the law and the Gentiles in Acts it appears James, the leader, either changed his mind about keeping the Laws of Moses or was faced with the mass conversion of Gentiles as a new phenomenon led by Paul. This evolution of insight was due to the fact God saved Gentiles who were not keeping the laws. It did not change the message from the Jewish leaders as to who Jesus was and what his mission was, to the Jews and now to the Gentiles. Even though the Gentiles need not keep the law, they must express their faith through a set of actions.

The placement of the Didache in history can be based on the following facts:
• When it was written churches were still being led by traveling teachers and prophets.
• In its instructions on the appointment of church leaders it mentions only two classes: bishops and deacons.
• Baptisms are still normally performed in rivers and streams.
• Prophets still preside at the Eucharist.
• The Eucharist or communion is still celebrated in conjunction with the agape or love feast.
• There is an absence of any theological dogma or discussion.

The range is wide in the speculation of the dates for the Didache, between 50 and 100 C.E.

There are clues that the author (or authors) of the Didache were close to either Jesus, or possibly the understudy of an Apostle. The author clearly shared in Jesus' opinion of the Pharisees as hypocrites (8:1). The author also had intimate knowledge of the Gospel of Matthew, or the "Q" source.

No intact copy of "Q" has ever been found. No reference to the document in early Christian writings has survived. Its existence is inferred from an analysis of the text of Matthew and Luke. Much of the content of Matthew and Luke was derived from the Gospel of Mark. But there were also many passages which appear to have come from another source document called the "Q" document.

Theologians and religious historians believe the Q's text can be reconstructed by analyzing passages that Matthew and Luke have in common. The first part of Q had to be written much earlier than the four canonical gospels of Mark, Matthew, Luke and John since there are identical passages in Mathew and Luke supplied by Q and Mark is influenced by the earliest part of Q. The earliest of the 40 or more gospels that were written and used by the early Christian movements may have traces of Q in them. These circulated before the controlling faction established what was to be orthodoxy and selected the books which were to become canon.

The Gospel of Q is different from the canonical gospels in that it does not extensively describe events in the life of Jesus. Rather, it is largely a collection of sayings -- similar to the Gospel of Thomas (see "the Gospel of Thomas by Joseph Lumpkin, published by Fifth Estate). Q does not mention the events of Jesus' virgin birth, his selection of 12 disciples, crucifixion, resurrection, or ascension to heaven. It represents those parts of Jesus' teachings that his followers remembered and recorded about 20 years after his death. Jesus is presented as a charismatic teacher, a healer, a simple man filled with the spirit of God. Jesus is also a sage, the personification of Wisdom, and the servant of God.

Through analysis of Matthew and Luke it is possible to draw out those verses that are identical, word for word, suggesting it was not an oral tradition relying on memory, but was a written source used by both Matthew and Luke.

By putting together the Didache and "Q" we have a view of the gospel and the doctrine of the young church and a glimpse into the heart of the first Christians.

The earliest Christian preaching about Jesus was not concerned abou his death and resurrection. It was only later that the early Church turned its attention to the chronology and events of the rest of the life of Jesus.

It was the resurrection that was the most important event in Christianity, especially for the earliest Christians. The resurrection was God's stamp of approval on the messiah. It was the power of God coming upon his good and faithful servant that raised him up as a sign for the people that this was indeed the real anointed one, the real Christ, the real messiah. The resurrection left no doubt.

Early Christians were hardly monolithic in their preachings and it was not until the 2nd century C.E. that the concept of the virgin birth of Jesus took hold. Critics of the virgin birth claim the concept was taken from pagan religions such as Mithaism, a mystery religion practiced in Rome between the first and fourth centuries C.E. Other critics claim the virgin birth was a counter claim to the Jewish slander of the illegitimate birth of Jesus. However, since both Matthew and Luke attest to the event it is supported by two witnesses, but this is only two of the four gospels. Such a miraculous event would likely be recorded by all.

There is speculation the Didache is a collaborative work of some council members as a proposed draft for the letter finally sent to outline under what conditions and through what teaching and by what initiation could a Gentile become a Christian (Acts 15:22-29). James would have been the main contributor as the leader. This seems to be supported by the key points made in Chapters 1-6, which elaborate on the more simplified points that were made in the final letter. Some instruction (4:8, 6:3, 8:8) also appears to overlap with events in early chapters of Acts, and there is also some terminology used during the time of Acts, such as *your servant, Jesus* (9:3, 9:5, 10:3), and one use of the term *Christian* (12:4). The letter would have gone out immediately while Acts would have been penned later.

The Didache falls into three parts. The first part (Chapters 1-6) is a moral treatise describing the Two Ways, the Way of Life and the Way of Death. The second and third parts contain instructions on baptism, the Eucharist, fasting, prayer, matters of church organization for the positions of apostles, teachers, prophets, bishops, and deacons.

It is perhaps the first text to append a doxology to the Lord's Prayer "...for thine is the power and the glory unto all ages." This doxology was picked up by the church and is now part of the Lord's Prayer for the Protestant churches. The words "the kingdom" were added later and are preserved in the document "The Apostolic Constitutions". The Textus Receptus, from which the King James Version was translated, included many references to a "didache" or teaching of the apostles, and several quotes from the didache, such as the longer version of the Lord's Prayer.

The "Our Father" is contained twice in the Bible (Matt. 6:9-13; Luke 11:2-4) with no doxology. In fact no doxology is found in the older manuscripts. The doxology is simply a prayer from the believers whose spirits were moved to close the prayer with deep reverence.

The normal practice in Judaism was for the person praying to add his own requests and doxology to a prayer that did not already have a fixed conclusion. The fact that the Lord's Prayer ends abruptly explains why early Jewish Christians may have felt the prayer required a personal conclusion. Tertullian confirms that in his day the practice was for worshippers to append their own petitions to the Lord's Prayer.

Egypt and Syria both have claims as the place of origin for the Didache. The case for Egypt was put forward because Clement of Alexadria, an early witness, stated it was very popular in Egypt, in the fourth century. He based this on Anthanasius The Great's reference to it and the numerous Coptic and Ethiopian versions available. The case for Syria is in the text on ministry and the apostolic decree of Acts 15:23-9 describing characteristic of early Syrian Christianity. The text in chapter 6 suggests a large but rural community, like that of Syria rather than the more metropolitan Egypt.

The Didache should not be confused with the *"Didascalia Apostolorum"*, *"Teaching of the Twelve Holy Apostles and Disciples of Our Savior,"* a 3rd century text founded upon the *Didache. The Didache* is the foundation of the Didascalia, which is an expanded version of the Didache.

The Didascalia continues to be part of the canon of the Ethiopic Christian church called the "Broader Canon."

The Didache is the earliest Orthodox Christian writing we have that is not contained in the New Testament and likely predates most of the writings contained in the New Testament.

Because it predates so much of the New Testament, it predates the idea of Sola Scriptura, the idea that the Bible contains all knowledge needed for salvation. Not only was Sola Scriptura unknown, it would have been impossible. There was no New Testament to point to as scripture. No Scriptura - no Sola Scriptura.

The Didache is a witness to the early Church of the Apostolic Age, and is evidence that the Faith of the Orthodox Church today is much the same as that of Christians of those times.

The original is a composite text. One of the earliest copies is known as the Jerusalem manuscript. It seems to be a reliable copy and was written at the close of the first century. If it is a culmination of the evolutionary process, then the texts or ideas backing this text must have emerged earlier. This would put the date of the ideas so far back as to coincide with the period of the earliest Jewish converts to the sect of the Nazarene.

The texts have evolved over a considerable period, from its beginning as a Jewish catechetical work, which was taken up and developed by the Church into a manual of Church life and order. The text was repeatedly modified in line with changes in the practice of the people of the communities who used it. The core of chapters 1 - 6 is Jewish and pre-Christian (ca. 100 B.C.E. to 50 C.E.) but this is to be expected since early Christianity was a sect of Judaism and thus followed basic Jewish religious practices. As a whole the text reached its present form by the end of the first century C.E.

There exists an eleventh century manuscript bearing the names "The Didache" and "The Teaching of the Twelve Apostles" ("Didache ton dodeka apostolon"). These are not the same texts, although the latter is an expansion of the first.

The Jerusalem manuscript was discovered in 1873 by Greek Orthodox Archbishop Philotheos Bryennios, Metropolitan of Nicomedia, in the library of the patriarch of Jerusalem at Constantinople. It is a clear and accurate copy made by a man called Leo, "scribe & sinner", dated to the year 1056 C.E. In 1883, Byrennios translated the manuscript, with introduction and comments. He correctly identified the Didache as the product of a Jewish Christian community.

A couple of years later, an Ethiopian version of the Didache was found and then published by Horner in 1904. Greek & Coptic fragments were discovered among the Oxyrhynchus Papyri. In 1992 the Greek version was published, followed by the Coptic version in 1924.

The Greek version of the Didache is contained in this book.

 The text as we have it today can be divided into four evolutionary phases:

(1) The original text (ca. 50-100 C.E.) : the first century original;

(2) The composite versions of the text in view of the needs of a particular Jewish Christian community ;

(3) The oldest extant independent and complete manuscripts of such a composite version. The Jerusalem manuscript is a 1056 copy and bears two titles. The text has a composition that does not flow, as it shifts from the writing style of one person to another, but it has a unity of the composition. It is clearly the product of a joint effort, containing mid second century additions or changes;

(4) The critical text : 21th century translation and interpretation with consideration given to all known documents, such as the Jerusalem manuscripts, the Latin and Ethiopian versions, and the Greek and Coptic fragments.

Harnack argues that the completed Didache originated in a backward community in rural Egypt around 140-165 C.E., whereas Sabatier claims a mid first century redaction (or earlier), in Syria. Recently, Mack situated the text in Galilea, about 100 C.E. Others claim 50 – 100 C.E. Hence, the precise date and place of origin of the original text remains a matter of debate, although a first century original is very likely. Judging from the form of the prayers and how they follow Jewish customs, the text must have been written in the time before pagan followers and influences began to be introduced, and well before the time when Christianity began to diverge from its Jewish roots.

There is a dualistic approach to logic and teaching in the text. Even though this is seen in Old Testament books such as Proverbs the approach in the Didache is not the short, two sentence type found there but more of the dualism or binary logic taught by the Greeks. There is no reason to think that the form of the Two Ways tradition shared by Barnabas and the Didache were from Semitic Judaism. The form seems more the type that flourished in the Greek schools of Hellenistic Judaism and philosophy for decades, if not centuries. Early Christian writers later came to adopt it. Two Ways theme in the Didache is almost exclusively limited to Didache 1.1-6.2. The Two Way approach is absent from Didache 6.3-15.4. This shows evidence of additions and evolutions.

It is possible that some connection once existed between the Didache and a Two Ways tradition presented in Barnabas. Some material present in the Two Ways can also be seen in Hermas, Similitudes 9.26.3. It is difficult to say with certainty which came first, but it is likely that Barnabas borrowed freely from the approach or presentation style of the Didache.

The strong Jewish influence, emphasis on leadership, prophecy, baptism and liturgies based around the Eucharistic along with the belief in the immediate return of Jesus Christ as the foundation of spiritual and communal life all imply that it was part of the earliest stage of the development of the myth of Christ, which apparently set in very rapidly after Jesus died or departed.

If the original, or core text was written before 100 C.E. but after the destruction of the second Temple in 70 C.E. it would situate the original Didache in the period of 70-100 C.E. The text contains material pertaining to first century Jewish concepts and its "two way" morality, which point to the Qumran community and the earliest forms of "Christianity" with what we now recognize as baptism and thanksgiving. However, since we know the Qumran community was in place a century before, and was an apocalyptic sect it is no proof of date.

There is a reference to "the Name of the Father, the Son and the Holy Spirit" in the ceremony of baptism, but the place and purpose of each "member" is not defined. The formula for baptism should not be read as Trinitarian since the divinity of Jesus was not accepted by most Jews, even some Christian Jews. It is probably a later interpolation placed upon the text. Nowhere else is the "Son" invoked (except in His apocalyptic station - 16:4), and nowhere is the identity of Jesus as the "Son of God" clearly and explicitly made.

The Didache, together with the epistles, were read during worship by the sect called Judeo-Christians. It was often cited by the Church Fathers. Some of them placed it next to the New Testament. As an overview of the major points, let us look at Baptism, Fasting, and the Eucharist.

Baptism:

"But concerning baptism, thus shall ye baptize. Having first recited all these things, baptize in the name of the Father and of the Son and of the Holy Spirit in living [running] water. But if thou hast not living water, then baptize in other water; and if thou art not able in cold, then in warm. But if thou hast neither, then pour water on the head thrice in the name of the Father and of the Son and of the Holy Spirit. But before the baptism let him that baptizes and him that is baptized fast, and any others also who are able; and thou

shalt order him that is baptized to fast a day or two before."
- Didache, 7:1-7

The early Christian practices of Baptism via triple immersion and fasting before Baptism are still preserved in the Orthodox Church today.

Fasting:

"And let not your fastings be with the hypocrites [Jews], for they fast on the second [Monday] and the fifth [Thursday] day of the week; but do ye keep your fast on the fourth [Wednesday] and on the preparation [the sixth -- Friday] day." - Didache, 8:1-2

Eucharist:

"But let no one eat or drink of this eucharistic thanksgiving, but they that have been baptized into the name of the Lord; for concerning this also the Lord hath said: Give not that which is holy to the dogs."
Didache, 9:10-12

The Didache has many similarities to other epistles written around the same time. These epistles are:

1st Epistle of Clement to the Corinthians (ca. 96) is a formal letter sent by the church of Rome to the church of Corinth as a result of trouble there that had led to the disposition of presbyters. Clement urges the Christians of Corinth (rebelling against church authority) to be submissive and obedient. Tradition attributes it to Clement, the first bishop of Rome who claimed catholic authority.

The Epistle of Barnabas (ca. 130) is a letter written to repudiate the claims of Jewish Christians who advocated adhering to the observance of the Law of Moses.

The Shepherd of Hermas (ca. 150) is an apocalyptic text written by Hermas, who is believed to be brother of Pius, the bishop of Rome. Practical matters of church purity and discipline in the second century come to the fore.

The Epistle of Polycarp to the Philippians (ca. 130) was a church leader (bishop) in Smyrna, Asia Minor. He exhorted the Philippians to holy living, good works and unmovable faith. He was interested in ministry and practical aspects of the daily life of Christians.

The Martyrdom of Polycarp is the earliest preserved story of Christian martyrs, probably from the last part of the second century. It records the trial and execution of Polycarp, who was burned at the stake.

The writings of Ignatius, who was the bishop of Antioch in Syria martyred in Rome by beasts in the beginning of the second century. On his way to Rome, he visited and then wrote to various churches, warning and exhorting them. He also wrote to Rome, and to Polycarp, bishop of Smyrna. He warned the church against heresies that threatened peace and unity. He opposed Gnosticism and Docetism. He penned letters to the Ephesians, Magnesians, Trallians, Romans, Philadelphians, Smyrnaeans and a letter to Polycarp.

In a time when Jewish Christianity was less refined and organized and followers were faced with defining the major elements of the emergent Christian faith, it was the Didache that offered the first text book of worship. Importance is given to the way of life, to prophecy, to communal gatherings, to the apocalypse, and to the soon return of Jesus.

"Jesus Christ" is only mentioned once, during the rite of broken bread (9:3-4). The sharing of eucharistic bread is not the reason for the gathering. There is no mention of the one body of Christ (1 Corinthians, 10:17). The breaking of bread is a foretaste and anticipation of the return of Christ and the perfection of self and community his return will bring, when all are united, and the "end time" brings restoration of holiness, peace, and complete harmony with God and His followers.

Christ is not mentioned during the rite of cup (9:2), neither does this title appear in the communal thanksgiving prayer, which is offered after the meal.

During the eucharist (9:2-3, 10:2-3) Jesus is called "servant" (Greek "pais") of the Father and "Christ" (annionted) only once and his connection with the "broken bread" is referenced in 9:4.

The early Christian community believed the beginning of the "end time" and the coming apocalypse was heralded with the arrival and death of Jesus. It is the space of time between then and the return of Jesus that we deal with here.

In the Didache, the traditional Jewish custom of drinking wine, breaking bread and saying thanks after the meal was not made referring to Christ nor was the meal or thanksgiving looking to the relationship between bread and wine and the Body and Blood of the "Son of God". The love-meal (agape) was rooted in the eucharist but became isolated only after the ritual meal of Judaism and the eucharist were separated. At the time there were many pagan religions conducting rituals in which there was symbolic eating of the "flesh" of a sacrificial victim or "god". The ceremony was common throughout the Middle East with the mystery cults, Mithraism, Isis and Osiris, Greek mysteries and other religious festivals. The rituals proposed in the Didache are not about this pagan practice but are firmly rooted in the tradition of Jewish prayer and community. Didache 10 is suggestive of the "birkat ha-mazon", a thanksgiving prayer at the end of the Jewish supper.

There is no mention that Christ is god who came in the flesh and died on the cross for our sins. This notion became the basis for the Christian Mass later.

(It should be noted, as odd as it may seem to modern Christians, that there were those who believed that Jesus was born of a virgin but still rejected his divinity. One idea does not follow the other.)

The disagreement between Eastern and Western Christianity as to the precise moment that consecration of the host happens within the Mass (both positions being without empirical proof) caused a schism between Eastern and Western Christianity. The West believes at the mention of "the Son" there is consecration (and transubstantiation), whereas the East invokes the Holy Spirit to effect the change of the substances of the Eucharist.

There are traces of Q-material in the Didache, which indicates the Didache is independent of the seed document Matthew and Luke drew upon, which most believe was the Gospel of Mark. Mathew and Luke added the full Q material to Mark. Perhaps the Didache helps to explain the background behind the gospel texts. The Didache suggests an independence from the synoptic Gospels and so throws light on the text of these gospels. This may confirm that the sayings of Jesus were collected in a written form. These saying were later placed into a document containing over one hundred sayings of Jesus, producing "Q" and "The Gospel of Thomas." Like the Didache, the Gospel of Thomas is not a narrative gospel but a wisdom discourse.

The information within the text is presented as a wisdom book based on the sayings of Jesus, which is in the Q document, instead of the narrative gospels, which tell a story. There is a parallel between Didache 9:5 where a logia is mentioned and the Gospel of Thomas.

If we examine what became the Lord's Prayer we find it fairly intact.
"When you pray, say :
'Father, may Your Name be holy.
May Your rule take place.
Always give us our bread.
Forgive us our debts,
for we ourselves forgive everyone that is indebted to us.
And lead us away from a trying situation'."
Q1, logia 42-44.

The word "epiousios" (8:2) is usually translated as "daily". This translation is somewhat arbitrary but became ubiquitous and thus the accepted rendering. The word "epiousion" has "epi" and "ousia as its parts. Epi means, "it is present" or "it happens". "Ousia" means "substance or essence". It refers to the "bread". If "epiousion" is understood as a "spiritual" process happening with the bread, then this word can be read as, "Give us now our spiritual bread."

The early Christians believed that Christ would come back within their lifetime. Their liturgies served to remind them of the imminent return. The love feast or Eucharist was not part of His death as it is today. There was no interpretation of "bread" as the "Body of Christ", nor is there a trace of the "this is My body" - "this is My blood". The meal - the Eucharist - was a gathering and a meal as a rehearsal and reminder of what communal unity and love was to come. To experience the presence of Christ by anticipating his return is evidenced in the Didache. This is the only text we have containing liturgical information about the Q-communities, of which the Essenes belonged.

The Didache shows little to no "Pauline" Christianity. Paul would have been present but his influence had not yet been fully established. It was James, the brother of Jesus, who was the "heir apparent" after the death of Jesus. James headed the Jewish Christian movement. Although Peter may have had a high status it was James who became the head of the Christian church or ministry in Jerusalem, which was considered the holiest position at the time. James wished to continue closer to the line of Judaism but Paul wished to reach out to the Pagan Gentile population. Later, the Catholic Church would view Peter as the apostle of succession and attempt to trace the papal lineage back to him, however Paul, it seems, had the greatest influence on Christianity and much of our faith today is Christianity as interpreted by Paul.

In the Book of Acts we are told Paul and Barnabas came back to Jerusalem to speak to the Apostles. The apostles, led by James, gave them a list of things to do. It was an odd list. Acts 15:*29 You are to abstain from food sacrificed to idols, from blood, from the meat of strangled animals and from sexual immorality. You will do well to avoid these things.*
    Farewell.

The major problem between Jews and the Gentile converts had to do with the Gentile's continuation to worship their idols and act according to that worship instead of the Christian way. All recommendations have a connection with pagan idol worship, of which sex acts and various forms of animal sacrifice and feast were part.

Ex 20:2-6

2 I am the LORD your God, who brought you out of Egypt, out of the land of slavery.

3 You shall have no other gods before me.

4 You shall not make for yourself an idol in the form of anything in heaven above or on the earth beneath or in the waters below.

5You shall not bow down to them or worship them; for I, the LORD your God, am a jealous God, punishing the children for the sin of the fathers to the third and fourth generation of those who hate me,

6but showing love to a thousand [generations] of those who love me and keep my commandments.

Other "suggestions" are based on the 7th commandment and the Gentile's immorality. This is because such immorality was connected to idol worship.

Ex 20:14

"You shall not commit adultery.

The list of restrictions aimed at the Gentiles addressed only the major issues so the other commandments were not discussed. The Gentiles were not given license to break the other commandments. It was simply that those other offenses were not an issue.

All recommendations were based on common practices among the Gentiles who were recently converted. Gentiles couldn't consume food and drinks of close friends and relatives who sacrificed to idols.

Gentiles did not have to be circumcised to prove that they were Christians, but they had to avoid continuing certain practices. In other words, Gentile Christians should not have to become officially like their Jewish brethren through circumcision, but they should avoid identifying themselves as pagans through practices.

In the early days of Christianity the movement was considered an offshoot sect of Judaism. Soon the main trunk of the sect began to split into three major branches, although even these main branches soon began to splinter. We will first look at the main divisions and discuss the minor differences within the subdivisions later.

The Didache captures a snapshot of Christianity before it was infiltrated with the pagan religions, which surrounded the areas of Christian concentration, Jerusalem and Rome.

One of the main influences was the religion of Mithras. Virtually all of the elements of Orthodox Christian rituals, from miter, wafer, water baptism, alter, and doxology, were adopted from the Mithras and earlier pagan mystery religions. The religion of Mithras preceded Christianity by roughly six hundred years. However, it was very active in Rome from the 1st to 4th centuries C.E.

(1) According to the Mithras myth, Mithras was born on December 25th as an offspring of the Sun. Next to the gods Ormuzd and Ahrimanes, Mithras held the highest rank among the gods of ancient Persia. He was represented as a beautiful youth and a Mediator. Reverend J. W. Lake states: "Mithras is spiritual light contending with spiritual darkness, and through his labors the kingdom of darkness shall be lit with heaven's own light; the Eternal will receive all things back into his favor, the world will be redeemed to God. The impure are to be purified, and the evil made good, through the mediation of Mithras, the reconciler of Ormuzd and Ahriman. Mithras is the Good, his name is Love. In

relation to the Eternal he is the source of grace, in relation to man he is the life-giver and mediator" (Plato, Philo, and Paul, p. 15).

(2) Mithras was considered a great teacher and master. He had twelve companions and traveled with performing miracles.

(3) Mithras was called "the good shepherd, "the way, the truth and the light, redeemer, savior, Messiah." He was identified with both the lion and the lamb.

(4) The International Encyclopedia states: "Mithras seems to have owed his prominence to the belief that he was the source of life, and could also redeem the souls of the dead into the better world ... The ceremonies included a sort of baptism to remove sins, anointing, and a sacred meal of bread and water, while a consecrated wine, believed to possess wonderful power, played a prominent part."

(5) Chambers Encyclopedia says: "The most important of his many festivals was his birthday, celebrated on the 25th of December, the day subsequently fixed -- against all evidence -- Baptism and the partaking of a mystical liquid,

consisting of flour and water, to be drunk with the utterance of sacred formulas, were among the inauguration acts."

(6) Prof. Franz Cumont, of the University of Ghent, writes as follows concerning the religion of Mithras and the religion of Christ: "Followers of Mithras also held Sunday sacred, and celebrated the birth of the Sun on the 25th of December...." (The Mysteries of Mithras, pp. 190, 191).

(7) Reverend Charles Biggs stated: "The disciples of Mithra formed an organized church, with a developed hierarchy. They possessed the ideas of Mediation, Atonement, and a Savior, who is human and yet divine, and not only the idea, but a doctrine of the future life. They had a Eucharist, and a Baptism, and other curious analogies might be pointed out between their system and the church of Christ (The Christian Platonists, p. 240).

(8) In Roman catacombs a relic of Mithraic worship was preserved. It was a picture of the infant Mithras seated in the lap of his virgin mother, while on their knees before him were Persian Magi adoring him and offering gifts.

(9) He was buried in a tomb and after three days he rose again. His resurrection was celebrated every year.

(10) The Christian Father Manes, founder of the heretical sect known as Manicheans, believed that Christ and Mithras were one. His teaching, according to Mosheim, was as follows: "Christ is that glorious intelligence which the Persians called Mithras ... His residence is in the sun" (Ecclesiastical History, 3rd century, Part 2, ch. 5).

We can see from the above list that there may have been a "cross-pollination" of stories and myths between religions. We must take care not to throw out truth simply because it is mimicked in paganism. Just because a pattern occurs in another religion, it does not make the pattern in Christianity incorrect. We must simply strip off the contamination to find the original and true belief system.

Above all, to discover the unsullied core of Christianity we dare not go past the Counsel of Nicaea. The Emperor Constantine was thought to be a follower of Mithras who adopted Christianity as a matter of expediency for the purpose of uniting and controlling his subjects, the majority of whom were Christian. While forging this unity he was active in the formation of modern Christian doctrines, such as the trinity. The creed produced under his watchful eye confirms several beliefs held by the followers of Mithras, and likely held by the emperor himself.

The Nicene Creed

When the Council of Nicaea **(C.E. 325)** rejected the teaching of Arius, it expressed its position by adopting one of the current Eastern symbols and inserting into it some anti-Arian phrases, resulting in this creed. At the Council of Constantinople **(C.E. 381)** some minor changes were made, and it was reaffirmed at the Council of Chalcedon **(C.E. 451).** It is an essential part of the doctrine and liturgy of the Lutheran churches. Historically it has been used especially at Holy Communion on Sundays and major feasts (except when the Apostles' Creed is used as the Baptismal Creed).

We believe in one God,
the Father, the Almighty,
maker of heaven and earth,
of all that is, seen and unseen.
We believe in one Lord, Jesus Christ,
the only Son of God,
eternally begotten of the Father,

God from God, Light from Light,

true God from true God,

begotten, not made,

of one Being with the Father.

Through Him all things were made.

For us and for our salvation

He came down from heaven;

by the power of the Holy Spirit

He became incarnate from the Virgin Mary, and was made man.

For our sake He was crucified under Pontius Pilate;

He suffered death and was buried.

On the third day He rose again

in accordance with the Scriptures;

He ascended into heaven

and is seated at the right hand of the Father.

He will come again in glory to judge the living and the dead,

and His kingdom will have no end.

We believe in the Holy Spirit, the Lord, the giver of life,

who proceeds from the Father and the Son.

With the Father and the Son He is worshiped and glorified.

He has spoken through the Prophets.

We believe in one holy catholic and apostolic Church.

We acknowledge one baptism for the forgiveness of sins.
We look for the resurrection of the dead,
and the life of the world to come. Amen.

Those who stayed with the roots of the Jesus movement were mostly Jewish converts. Many were still worshipping in synagogues. The Jewish Christians viewed it as their duty to love God and neighbor, serve the community, and pray for their enemies. They accepted Jesus as the anointed servant of God and the one sent to mediate between God and man (in the way a of a priest) and teach us how to live in order to please God, but they did not accept that Jesus was God, nor did the idea of his death paying for our sin occur to them. To this group it was their faith in God and following the teachings of Jesus regarding the way one treated others and loved God that was the path to salvation. Jesus was regarded as a man, pure and righteous enough that he could communicate with God and talk to the people. Thus, he was the mediator.

Another group who combined various Greek philosophies with the new faith were Gnostics. They believed this world was evil and the body entrapped the spirit. Salvation was realizing the truth that the material world was the enemy of the spiritual world. Jesus was sent to teach the people who the real God was and that the spirit world was the most important realm.

Then there was "Pauline Christianity." This is what the church practices today. James and most of the other apostles did not subscribe to many of Paul's interpretations of Christianity. Paul had never met Jesus in the flesh and was a late-comer to the faith, although he claimed to have spent time in the desert where the ascended Jesus appeared and instructed him. Did Paul really know the intent of Jesus better than believers who grew up with him, such as his brother, who was now over the main Christian church? Paul taught that faith and faith alone brought salvation to the convert. The faith demanded was one focused on the fact that Jesus was sent by God to die in our place and thus take our place in the hands of a God who, without seeing such a faith would assign hell to those who violated the least of the Old Testament laws. Paul rejected the Old Testament laws and rituals for those who were saved. Did James and the others misunderstand exactly who and what Jesus was? Was Jesus, the prophet, without honor in his own land? Or, did Paul hijack Christianity by imposing his own interpretations of faith, grace, works, and redemption?

The spilling of blood and the sacrifice of Jesus as the payment of sin is not mentioned in the Didache. Jesus is the Messiah, the Christ, the anointed one, the servant of God, but not God in the flesh. The Holy Spirit is mentioned as the baptism is done in the name of the Father, Son, and Holy Spirit. This forces us to discern the difference between the Spirit of God and God, who is a spirit.

The Didache gives simple instruction to the initiates for their entrance into the community and their salvation:

Show love toward your neighbor and enemies.

Abstain from lusts.

Give to the needy and show compassion to others.

Do not murder, Do not commit adultery, Do not have illicit sex, Do not steal, Do not commit abortion or infanticide.

Do not be prone to anger.

Do not engage in sorcery, witchcraft, enchanting, astrology. (This refers to potions, drugs, spells, dealing with spirits of the dead or evil spirits, or attempting to foretell the future.)

Share all things with your brothers and sisters.

Do not eat food that was sacrificed to idols.

Baptize in living (running, fresh) water in the name of the Father, Son and Holy Spirit.

Fast on the 4th day of the week.

Recite the Our Father prayer three times a day.

Beware of and reject false prophets.

Elect honorable Christians to be bishops and deacons to oversee the members.

Be ready at all times for the return of Jesus, who is the servant of God and the mediator who came to teach us how to live, worship, and commune.

The Didache gives instructions on certain ceremonies. Within the ceremonies of the Eucharist and thanksgiving the place of Jesus in the early church is shown. The cup is first consecrated. Nowhere is the divinity of Jesus Christ mentioned during the Offertory or the Eucharistic prayer. Jesus is only spoken of as "Christ" over the bread, not over the cup. Communion happens before thanksgiving. Thanksgiving does not ask for the consecration of the fully prepared elements since they are no longer present, having been already consumed. Thanksgiving is fully focused on God the Father. Jesus is not mentioned as Christ, nor as Son, but only as a servant of the Father God. Jesus returns to complete the work of gathering and unifying believers in holy peace and communion with God and one another.

In the Dead Sea Scrolls found at Qumrân, we find the following interesting text:

"And when they shall gather for the common table, to eat and to drink new wine, when the common table shall be set for eating and new wine poured for drinking, let no man extend his hand over the first-fruits of bread and wine before the Priest; for it is he who shall bless the first-fruits of bread and wine, and shall be the first to extend his hand over the bread. Thereafter, the Messiah of Israel shall extend his hand over the bread, and all the congregation of the Community shall utter a blessing, each man in the order of his dignity."

The Messianic Rule (1QSa) - translated by Vermes, 1990.

The Didache proves the early Christians believed faith and salvation can exist without the sacrifice of Jesus Christ for our sins. If he was not God he could not be totally perfect. If he was not divinely perfect he would have been an imperfect sacrifice. He was a man, though righteous. During the Eucharist, no mention is made of the sacrifice of Jesus Christ. Only the presence of Christ is needed to raise us spiritually. The idea of Jesus the Christ as the Son of God is not necessary. Jesus is a mediator who serves the Father. It is to God that all of us return and not to Christ. The title of the "Son of God" is used in the Didache when referring to deceivers and in the "Q" when Satan addresses Jesus. The title "Lord" does not justify the trinitarian identification or belief of Jesus Christ as God. This is far too early to entertain the ideas which evolved into the Nicean trinitarian doctrine. The title of "Lord" is used as one of respect. This will be explained in more depth later.

Thanksgiving is directed toward God, the Father, only. It is His Name which the Didache places in the middle. The cup and the "broken bread" refer to Jesus Christ, who is broken in the fashion of torture and murder but who unites his followers with love. His followers sense his return is imminent. He is always the mediator, never the principal subject. This idea is proven over and over again as we read the opening greetings of the Epistles (letters from one believer to another or a group). It is a greeting in the name of God the Father and the Lord Jesus.

Colossians 1
1Paul, an apostle of Jesus Christ by the will of God, and Timotheus our brother,

2To the saints and faithful brethren in Christ which are at Colosse: Grace be unto you, and peace, from God our Father and the Lord Jesus Christ.

1 Corinthians 1

1Paul called to be an apostle of Jesus Christ through the will of God, and Sosthenes our brother,

2Unto the church of God which is at Corinth, to them that are sanctified in Christ Jesus, called to be saints, with all that in every place call upon the name of Jesus Christ our Lord, both their's and our's:

3Grace be unto you, and peace, from God our Father, and from the Lord Jesus Christ.

2 Corinthians 1

1Paul, an apostle of Jesus Christ by the will of God, and Timothy our brother, unto the church of God which is at Corinth, with all the saints which are in all Achaia:

2Grace be to you and peace from God our Father, and from the Lord Jesus Christ.

1 Timothy 1

1Paul, an apostle of Jesus Christ by the commandment of God our Saviour, and Lord Jesus Christ, which is our hope;

2Unto Timothy, my own son in the faith: Grace, mercy, and peace, from God our Father and Jesus Christ our Lord.

2 Timothy 1

1Paul, an apostle of Jesus Christ by the will of God, according to the promise of life which is in Christ Jesus,
2To Timothy, my dearly beloved son: Grace, mercy, and peace, from God the Father and Christ Jesus our Lord.

James 1

1James, a servant of God and of the Lord Jesus Christ, to the twelve tribes which are scattered abroad, greeting.

Jude 1

1Jude, the servant of Jesus Christ, and brother of James, to them that are sanctified by God the Father, and preserved in Jesus Christ, and called:
2Mercy unto you, and peace, and love, be multiplied.

There does not seem to be any trinity here. He was not equal to God. With the exception of the Gospel of John (Jn. 20:28) apostles called Jesus "Lord", not "God". There is evidence that the Gospel of John was written latter (c.a.100C.E.) than the others and was influenced and changed. One may argue that the Gospel is different than the others due to hindsight and a more full revelation, or one may say the difference indicates corruption. Several books have been written arguing that John's Gospel has been changed to communicate trinity and divinity, which were not there in the original intent or wording. The Didache was written many years prior and did not yet attach divinity to Jesus.

The title of "Lord" is an antiquated term used by the translators in 1611 to render a word "kurios" from "kuros" meaning "The owner or controller of a person, a state sovereign, a title of honor such as "Sir". It has continued to indicate a higher spiritual status ever since.

The members of the community who used the Didache were Jewish Christians since they believed Jesus was the servant or anointed one sent from God. For them Jesus Christ saved them when he was anointed and sent as a "servant" of the Father, but not as God Himself. He was a mediator sent from God to teach and lead, not as the propitiation, as we now believe.

They saw no Trinity and no sacrificial Lamb of God. These first Christians saw Jesus as a servant doing the will of his master and carrying out the orders to teach, unite, mediate, and demonstrate the ideals of a godly life. Here, in the Didache, we see the beginnings and foundation of what men have built into the Christianity of today. It is the structure beneath the gilding.

Why was the teaching of the blood sacrifice of Jesus left out? Why is there no mention of his payment for the remission of our sins? Does the Didache present a salvation founded solely on works? Faith in God is accounted to the believer as righteousness through God's grace. By faith are we saved through grace. Doing the will of God as taught and exemplified by Jesus not only proves and demonstrates our faith, it completes it, fulfils it, and through discipline and the establishment of holy habits the person is changed and strengthened toward unwavering faith.

The relationship between faith and work is explained in detail throughout the Book of James.

James 2:20-24

Common English Bible (CEB)

20 Are you so slow? Do you need to be shown that faith without actions has no value at all? 21 What about Abraham, our father? Wasn't he shown to be righteous through his actions when he offered his son Isaac on the altar? 22 See, his faith was at work along with his actions. In fact, his faith was made complete by his faithful actions. 23 So the scripture was fulfilled that says, Abraham believed God, and God regarded him as righteous.[a] What is more, Abraham was called God's friend. 24 So you see that a person is shown to be righteous through faithful actions and not through faith alone.

James asked the only relevant question left.

James 2:14

New King James Version (NKJV)

Faith Without Works Is Dead

14 What does it profit, my brethren, if someone says he has faith but does not have works? Can faith save him?

And in another version it reads:

James 2:14

GOD'S WORD Translation (GW)

We Show Our Faith by What We Do

*   **14***My brothers and sisters, what good does it do if someone claims to have faith but doesn't do any good things? Can this kind of faith save him?*

Does this mean that salvation is not by faith alone? One may argue that if faith without works is dead and meaningless, then it would take both. Thus, according to James there is no Sola Fida (Faith Alone). Now, Sola Scriptura cannot be, for the early Christians are saved, not having the New Testament and Gentiles having neither Old or New Testaments are saved simply by accepting and following Jesus; and Sola Fida falls to the need for works to fulfill it, leaving only Sola Gratia (by Grace alone), for only through God's grace can our faith and acts be accounted to us as righteousness. No amount of work is worth heaven, but by grace our faith blooms into works and God's grace does the rest. As Isaiah 58 says, "All our righteousness are as filthy rags." This is the way the first Christians saw salvation.

Since the beginning of the Christian faith men have fought with themselves and one another to understand the position of faith and works within salvation. Martin Luther was so upset at the stance James took that he rejected the Epistle, calling it a "straw epistle", which he wanted to burn. The only two beliefs constituting the core of all mainstream forms of the faith were the resurrection and the return of Jesus.

In these ideas the Didache and the Book of James walks hand in hand to such a degree that it suggests that James himself, or one of his disciples, could have written Didache 1 – 6. So close is the parallel with the Didache that The Book of James is included in this book for the reader to compare after reading the first 6 chapters of the Didache for a fuller understanding of the Book of James.

Many scholars consider the epistle of James to be written in the late 1st or early 2nd centuries, after the death of James the Just. It is thought James may have written a prior version of the letter, which was later polished and completed by one of his disciples. James, being both the leader of the faith and one of the main contributors to the Didache, as the name "The Teaching if the Twelve" indicates, would have helped set the tone of the document. This theory is bolstered by the fact that the Book of James and the Didache are so similar is content. The other apostles, Peter, John, Andrew, James, Matthew, Simon,

Thomas, Jude, Philip, James the Less, Bartholomew, and Mathias would have contributed and all would have agreed with the teachings. Paul was not a contributor but came later, taking the title, "Apostle to the Gentiles," a title of specificity, which through circumstance and "mission creep" possibly took on a broader scope in the early church than first intended.

There are parallels between James, 1 Peter, 1 Clement and The Shepherd of Hermas reflecting the political situations Christians were dealing with in the 1st or early 2nd century.

Christianity at the time was primitive and in flux. There were already several sects of Christianity either established or evolving, each having a different idea of who Jesus was. We have discussed three major divisions. Now let us look at others. In the very early days of Christianity, there appear to have been:

Ebionites, meaning "the Poor Ones". They were an early Jewish Christian sect that lived around Judea from the 1st to the 4th century. This sect of Judæo-Christians believed Jesus was the messiah but they denied his divinity and supernatural origin. They observed all the Jewish rites, such as circumcision and the seventh-day Sabbath and they used the gospel according to Matthew written in Hebrew or Aramaic, but they flatly rejected the writings of Paul as those of an apostate. Some Ebionites accepted the doctrine of the virgin birth of Jesus. Most others did not.

Nazarene means "a Branch". They were an early Jewish Christian sect similar to the Ebionite. They accepted the virgin birth and divinity of Jesus. The term Nazarene was likely the one first used for these followers of Jesus, as evidenced by Acts 24:5 where Paul is called "the ringleader of the sect of the Nazarenes." Thus, these followers were likely folded into the Pauline sect later as Paul continues to develop his Christology. It was at this time that Paul's theology diverged enough from the first Jewish Christians that they discontinued use of the Didache.

The term "Christian," first used in Greek speaking areas for the movement is a translation of the term Nazarene, and basically means a "Messianist."

The Essenes, meaning "Doers of Torah", were the sect which wrote or collected the Dead Sea Scrolls. They were considered part of the collective term called "Way," and existed over 150 years before the birth of Jesus. They baptized as a sign of repentance as entrance requirement into their fellowship.

The Essenes were an apocalyptic group, expecting three redemptive Figures—the Prophet like Moses and his two Messiahs. The sect saw themselves as the remnant of God's people preparing the Way for the return of God's Glory. They formed a tight community and referred to themselves as brother and sister.

They had their own developed interpretation of Torah, some aspects of which Jesus preached. The ideas of no divorce, not using oaths, and the apocalypse are but a few. They followed one they called the True Teacher (Teacher of Righteousness) whom most scholars believe lived in the 1st century B.C.E. but was assassinated by the authorities of the time.

Nazoreans were a first century offshoot of the Essene, according to Epiphanius. There were two branches of Essenes - the Nazoreans and the Ossaeans. Each of these two Essene branches had a monastic part. The monastic part of the northern Nazorean was known as "Children of

Amen." The Nazorean B'nai-Amen were also a Monastic Order. It is thought that both Jesus and John the Baptizer were associated with the Essense and drew some of their doctrine and teachings from them.

Cerinthians followed the Jewish law, denied that the Supreme God had made the physical world, and denied the divinity of Jesus. The doctrine of Cerinthus is stated by Irenaeus in the following passage Ulcer. i. 26):

" A certain Cerinthus in Asia taught that the world was not made by the Supreme God, but by a certain power entirely separate and distinct from that authority which is above the universe, and ignorant of that God who is over all things. He submitted that Jesus was not born of a virgin (for this seemed to him impossible), but was the son of Joseph and Mary, born as all other men, yet excelling all mankind in righteousness, prudence, and wisdom. And that after His baptism there had descended on Him, from that authority which is above all things, Christ in the form of a dove; and that then He had announced the unknown Father and had worked miracles; but that at the end Christ had flown back again from Jesus, and that Jesus suffered and rose again, but that Christ remained impassible, since He was a spiritual being " (as quoted by A. S. Peake).

Hippolytus adds that Cerinthus taught that the world was made by an angel, and that the Law was given to the Jews by another angel, who was the God of the Jews. These angels were far below the Supreme Being. The teaching of Cerinthus is a mixture of Judaism and Gnosticism.

Carpocratians were an early Gnostic sect founded in the first half of the second century. Carpocrates venerated Jesus, but he also believed that the philosophers Plato, Pythagoras, Aristotle and others were gods. He believed that Jesus was just another man, like any of us, upon whom an extraordinary recollection descended. Carpocrates seems to have placed no faith in anything like the Immaculate Conception, or the virgin birth, but plainly states that Jesus was the son of Joseph. Essentially, Carpocretes believed there was no way to know anything more than what seems obvious.

The first gospels had only recently been written, or were still in the process of revision, but there was a sense that the writings were sacred, however they had not yet been granted canon. The Gnostics were writing their own scriptures. Why not? If there was a gospel written by Mark or Matthew why should there not be a gospel written by Thomas or Baranbas with a Gnostic slant? The Gnostics, being closer to the event of the formation of scripture were less trusting that what the four gospels contained was the untainted word of Christ. The possibility that Jesus was human, like anyone, did not disturb Carpocrates because he saw that the wisdom of Jesus had elevated him to godliness, which was therefore a possibility for anyone who emulated him, after all, Jesus did say we could do all that he did and more.

Carpocrates did not believe that salvation could be obtained only by following Jesus, but that one had to become Jesus (that is to be elevated to a higher spiritual level and become him in spirit) in order to find salvation.

Most Gnostics believed Jesus was the son of Joseph, and was just like other men, but his soul was steadfast and pure, he perfectly remembered those things which he had witnessed within the sphere of the Unbegotten God.

They respected Peter, Paul, and the rest of the apostles, whom they consider to be on an equal spiritual level to Jesus. The Gnostics believed the souls of Peter and Paul descended from the same sphere as that of Jesus.

Some would say that *Pauline Christianity*, with its distinctive theology, was a separate sect. Its followers were probably absorbed into the proto-Catholic-Orthodox sect early in the second century.

The *proto-Catholic-Orthodox* sect is believed to have coexisted with the above sects from the earliest times. Paul represents only one sect of early Christianity, each vying for converts and attempting to articulate their theology to the exclusion of the others. The Pauline sect was certainly not the "original" one. The original sect and the trunk from which all other sects formed was a messianic Judaism, guided by James. The earliest Christian sect was the Jewish Christianity practiced by Peter, James, and Jesus' earliest followers

Scholars agree Jesus, his family, his Twelve Apostles, the Elders, and his earliest followers observed the Torah and kept the laws, ceremonies and sacrifices, whereas the main feature of Paul's message was a rejection of the Torah and the Jewish law.

Acts chapter 15 suggests two things. It suggests that those who were Jews and converted to the Christian sect continued to practice according to their Jewish roots. It also suggests that even though the apostles gave leniency to the Gentiles, there were those within their group who did not wish to extend the same permission and continued to push the point that Gentiles should become Jews in order to be on equal footing with the apostles, following the Jewish footsteps of Jesus.

Paul's sect came to dominate Christianity partly through the circumstance of politics and partly because entry into the faith was easy, since it was through faith and not following the law. History is written by the winner, so we know little about other sects in earliest Christianity.

Jewish Christians considered Jesus the saving Messiah, but insisted on continued observance of the Jewish laws about ceremony, diet, and circumcision. To some Gentiles the required consent to mutilate their penis was simply too much.

As stated before, James seemed to be the heir apparent to the original Jewish sect of Christianity. James led the

Jerusalem church until the Jewish revolt of 66 CE. His commitment to the Torah is recorded by Josephus and by Acts 21:17-21.

The letter of James "to the twelve tribes of the Jewish diaspora" explains how faith produces the works and fruits. These works, which the Torah also demands has a saving function (Jas. 1:21). James mentions Jesus only twice, in incidental ways (1:1 and 2:1). However, James does define what he considers to be the sign of real faith.

Religion that is pure and genuine in the sight of God the Father will show itself by such things as visiting orphans and widows in their distress and keeping oneself uncontaminated by the world.
(James 1:27 Phiilip's translation)

Because Paul rejected the authority of the Torah, he wrote against Jewish Christians in 3 of his 7 undisputed letters. This is the main subject of Galatians, and he also warns against "dogs" who insist on circumcision in Phil. 3:2-3, and against those who take pride in their pedigree of being both "Hebrews" and "Israelites" in 2 Cor. 11:5 and 22-23. Paul rejected works as having no part in salvation, but instead insisted that only faith in Jesus could save a person's soul. This was an easier faith to enter and, until one was persecuted, it was an easier religion to live under, having fewer points by which one may be judged.

Yet, in all of this in-fighting, it was the timing of fate that may have decided the outcome of which sect would rule Christianity. The Jewish Christians fell victims to the war between Rome and the Jews and the aftermath that followed. Remembering the first sect of Christian Jews were still Jews by practice and continued to worship at the temple, when Rome attacked and slaughtered the Jews the population of Jewish Christians was reduced as well. Gentiles were not touched unless the Roman leaders knew they were Christians, since they considered Christians a sect of Judaism and political trouble-makers. Nero began his slaughter from 64 – 68 C.E.

The Jewish Virtual Library has this to say about the war: The Jews' Great Revolt against Rome in 66 C.E. led to one of the greatest catastrophes in Jewish life and, in retrospect, might well have been a terrible mistake.

No one could argue with the Jews for wanting to throw off

Roman rule. Since the Romans had first occupied Israel in 63 B.C.E.E., their rule had grown more and more onerous. From almost the beginning of the Common Era, Judea was ruled by Roman procurators, whose chief responsibility was to collect and deliver an annual tax to the empire. Whatever the procurators raised beyond the quota assigned, they could keep. Not surprisingly, they often imposed confiscatory taxes. Equally infuriating to the Judeans, Rome took over the appointment of the High Priest (a turn of events that the ancient Jews appreciated as much as modern Catholics would have appreciated Mussolini appointing the popes). As a result, the High Priests, who represented the Jews before God on their most sacred occasions, increasingly came from the ranks of Jews who collaborated with Rome.

At the beginning of the Common Era, a new group arose among the Jews: the Zealots. These anti-Roman rebels were active for more than six decades, and later instigated the Great Revolt. Their most basic belief was that all means were justified to attain political and religious liberty.

The Jews' anti-Roman feelings were seriously exacerbated during the reign of the half-crazed emperor Caligula, who in the year 39 C.E. declared himself to be a deity and ordered his statue to be set up at every temple in the Roman Empire. The Jews, alone in the empire, refused the command; they would not defile God's Temple with a statue of pagan Rome's newest deity.

Caligula threatened to destroy the Temple, so a delegation of Jews was sent to pacify him. To no avail. Caligula raged at them, "So you are the enemies of the gods, the only people who refuse to recognize my divinity." Only the emperor's sudden, violent death saved the Jews from wholesale massacre.

Caligula's action radicalized even the more moderate Jews. What assurance did they have, after all, that another Roman ruler would not arise and try to defile the Temple or destroy Judaism altogether? In addition, Caligula's sudden demise might also have been interpreted as confirming the Zealots' belief that God would fight alongside the Jews if only they would have the courage to confront Rome.

In the decades after Caligula's death, Jews found their religion subject to periodic gross indignities, Roman soldiers exposing themselves in the Temple on one occasion, and burning a Torah scroll on another.

Ultimately, the combination of financial exploitation, Rome's unbridled contempt for Judaism, and the unabashed favoritism that the Romans extended to Gentiles living in Israel brought about the revolt.

In the year 66 C.E., Florus, the last Roman procurator, stole vast quantities of silver from the Temple. The outraged Jewish masses rioted and wiped out the small Roman garrison stationed in Jerusalem. Cestius Gallus, the Roman ruler in neighboring Syria, sent in a larger force of soldiers. But the Jewish insurgents routed them as well.

This was a heartening victory that had a terrible consequence: Many Jews suddenly became convinced that they could defeat Rome, and the Zealots' ranks grew geometrically. Never again, however, did the Jews achieve so decisive a victory.

When the Romans returned, they had 60,000 heavily armed and highly professional troops. They launched their first attack against the Jewish state's most radicalized area of Galilee in the north. The Romans vanquished Galilee, and an estimated 100,000 Jews were killed or sold into slavery.

Throughout the Roman conquest of this territory, the Jewish leadership in Jerusalem did almost nothing to help their beleaguered brothers. They apparently had concluded—too late, unfortunately—that the revolt could not be won, and wanted to hold down Jewish deaths as much as possible.

The highly embittered refugees who succeeded in escaping the Galilean massacres fled to the last major Jewish stronghold—Jerusalem. There, they killed anyone in the Jewish leadership who was not as radical as they. Thus, all the more moderate Jewish leaders who headed the Jewish government at the revolt's beginning in 66 were dead by 68—and not one died at the hands of a Roman. All were killed by fellow Jews.

The scene was now set for the revolt's final catastrophe. Outside Jerusalem, Roman troops prepared to besiege the city; inside the city, the Jews were engaged in a suicidal civil war. In later generations, the rabbis hyperbolically declared that the revolt's failure, and the Temple's destruction, was due not to Roman military superiority but to causeless hatred (sinat khinam) among the Jews (Yoma 9b). While the Romans would have won the war in any case, the Jewish civil war both hastened their victory and immensely increased the casualties. One horrendous example: In expectation of a Roman siege, Jerusalem's Jews had stockpiled a supply of dry food that could have fed the city for many years. But one of the warring Zealot factions burned the entire supply, apparently hoping that destroying this "security blanket" would compel everyone to participate in the revolt. The starvation resulting from this mad act caused suffering as great as any the Romans inflicted.

We do know that some great figures of ancient Israel opposed the revolt, most notably Rabbi Yochanan ben Zakkai. Since the Zealot leaders ordered the execution of anyone advocating surrender to Rome, Rabbi Yochanan arranged for his disciples to smuggle him out of Jerusalem, disguised as a corpse. Once safe, he personally surrendered to the Roman general Vespasian, who granted him concessions that allowed Jewish communal life to continue.

During the summer of 70, the Romans breached the walls of Jerusalem, and initiated an orgy of violence and destruction. Shortly thereafter, they destroyed the Second Temple. This was the final and most devastating Roman blow against

Judea.

It is estimated that as many as one million Jews died in the Great Revolt against Rome. When people today speak of the almost two-thousand-year span of Jewish homelessness and exile, they are dating it from the failure of the revolt and the destruction of the Temple. Indeed, the Great Revolt of 66-70, followed some sixty years later by the Bar Kokhba revolt, were the greatest calamities in Jewish history prior to the Holocaust. In addition to the more than one million Jews killed, these failed rebellions led to the total loss of Jewish political authority in Israel until 1948. This loss in itself exacerbated the magnitude of later Jewish catastrophes, since it precluded Israel from being used as a refuge for the large numbers of Jews fleeing persecutions elsewhere.

SOURCE: Jewish Virtual Library. Solomon Zeitlin, The Rise and Fall of the Judean State, vol. 3.

Whether by propaganda, war, or the fact that pagans and Gentiles were converting to Pauline Christianity faster than the sect led by the followers of James, the Pauline sect soon became the dominant sect. Jewish Christianity remained influential and active for only a short time but the influence and theology is preserved in some early Christian writings that are as old as some books of the New Testament. Thet were not chosen for the New Testament canon since their theology went contrary to what became orthodoxy. 1 Clement, The Shepherd of Hermas, and The Didache are but a few of these books.

With the Jewish-Roman wars of 66 and 132 CE, the Jewish Temple was destroyed and Jewish Christians were scattered. Meanwhile Paul was having great success in his Gentile missions.

Paul's rejection of Jewish laws and ordinances, including circumcision made becoming a Christian very easy. The support and community within the group made becoming a Christian quite seductive to Gentiles, many of whom sought to become part of God's chosen people and partakers in the promises of Israel. Paul's message to the Gentiles included the followers of Jesus being grafted into the chosen people of God, they would then receive the blessings of Israel since most Jews has rejected Jesus as messiah, thus displeasing God.

By the fourth century, the Council of Nicea (backed by the

weight of the Roman Empire) and the formation of the New Testament canon decided forever what Christianity was, and it was not Jewish Christianity.

There was a one in three chance of the Pauline sect becoming the template of the Christianity of today. Had the Roman massacre of the Jews not happened or had Paul failed to convert enough Gentiles to his sect to outnumber those who followed James we could have a Messianic-Jewish based Christianity today. Our canon and our worship would be different, but because it would have been accepted, orthodox, and traditional, Christians would follow it as they follow the Pauline sect today. It is only by chance, or by the hand of god, that the Didache is not still in use as the main document of catechism today.

The Jewish Christians, led by James, had been looking for a Messiah who was a warrior-king. Although the Old Testament told of the torture and death of the messiah the church at this time was divided as to exactly who and what Jesus was. James dismissed the weighty matter of the death of Jesus as a sacrifice for the sins of the world. James, being a devout Jew was looking at Jesus from the Jewish viewpoint of what the Messiah was supposed to be.

According to Jewish scripture and belief, the true Messiah must meet the following requirements.

He must be an observant Jewish man descended from the house of King David.

He must be "The son of man" which is human as opposed to the Son of God.

He must bring peace to the world.

He must gather all Jews back into Israel. (This is usually thought to be through a war.)

He must rebuild the ancient Temple in Jerusalem.

He must convert the world and they will worship the God of Israel. This means observing the Torah and the Law.

The concept of the messiah seems to have developed in later Judaism. The Torah contains very few specific reference to him, though some Jewish scholars have pointed out that it does speak of the "End of Days," which is the time of the messiah.

The Tanakh gives several specifications as to who the messiah will be. He will be a descendent of King David (2 Samuel 7:12-13; Jeremiah 23:5), observant of Jewish law

(Isaiah 11:2-5), a righteous judge (Jeremiah 33:15), and a great military leader.

Jews do not believe that the messiah will be divine. A fundamental difference between Judaism and Christianity is the Jewish conviction that God is so essentially different and more holy than humanity that he could not become a human. The messiah is a servant, a man sent by God, a person of pure spirit who can hear from God and speak to mankind. If Jesus was or is God how could he say to us we could do greater works than he did? The fact that the modern church views Jesus as God has stifled believers from performing greater miracles. After all, who could do greater works than God? But if Jesus was a servant, we could be servants of God also and do the same works if not greater. Was this not his message, that we should be like him? He could not ask this of us if he was God.

Moreover, Jews find no foundation in the scriptures for belief in the divinity of the messiah. Passages viewed by Christians as indicating a divine messiah, such as the suffering servant of Isaiah 53, are viewed by Jews as speaking of the people of Israel en masse.

Isaiah 53

New International Version (NIV)

1 Who has believed our message and to whom has the arm of the LORD been revealed? 2 He grew up before him like a tender shoot, and like a root out of dry ground. He had no beauty or majesty to attract us to him, nothing in his appearance that we should desire him. 3 He was despised and rejected by mankind, a man of suffering, and familiar with pain. Like one from whom people hide their faces he was despised, and we held him in low esteem.

4 Surely he took up our pain and bore our suffering, yet we considered him punished by God, stricken by him, and afflicted. 5 But he was pierced for our transgressions, he was crushed for our iniquities; the punishment that brought us peace was on him, and by his wounds we are healed. 6 We all, like sheep, have gone astray, each of us has turned to our own way; and the LORD has laid on him the iniquity of us all.

7 He was oppressed and afflicted, yet he did not open his mouth; he was led like a lamb to the slaughter, and as a sheep before its shearers is silent, so he did not open his mouth. 8 By oppression and judgment he was taken away. Yet who of his generation protested? For he was cut off from the land of the living; for the transgression of my *people he was punished. **9** He was assigned a grave with the wicked, and with the rich in his death, though he had done no violence, nor was any deceit in his mouth.*

*   **10** Yet it was the LORD's will to crush him and cause him to suffer, and though the LORD makes his life an offering for sin, he will see his offspring and prolong his days, and the will of the LORD will prosper in his hand. **11** After he has suffered, he will see the light of life and be satisfied; by his knowledge my righteous servant will justify many,   and he will bear their iniquities. **12** Therefore I will give him a portion among the great, and he will divide the spoils with the strong, because he poured out his life unto death, and was numbered with the transgressors. For he bore the sin of many and made intercession for the transgressors.*

In Origen's writings, called "Contra Celsus," written in the year 248, he writes of Isaiah 53:

"Now I remember that, on one occasion, at a disputation held with certain Jews, who were reckoned wise men, I quoted these prophecies; to which my Jewish opponent replied, that these predictions bore reference to the whole people, regarded as one individual, and as being in a state of dispersion and suffering, in order that many proselytes might be gained, on account of the dispersion of the Jews among numerous heathen nations."

To the Jewish interpretation of the Torah these are the few scriptural references to the messiah.

Isaiah 2, 11, 42; 59:20 - Jeremiah 23, 30, 33; 48:47; 49:39 - Ezekiel 38:16 - Hosea 3:4-3:5 - Micah 4 - Zephaniah 3:9 - Zechariah 14:9 - Daniel 10:14.

Owing to the Jewish view of the messiah in the first century it is no wonder that the Didache does not mention the sacrifice of the messiah for the remission of sin.

It is possible the Didache reveals to us the earliest, most pure and simple form of a belief in Jesus as the Christ. There was no mention of the virgin birth, or divinity of Jesus. There is no thought of Jesus being a sacrificed for the payment of our sins. There was no rapture, or trinity. There is only a rock-solid belief in Jesus as the messiah sent as a servant of God to be the mediator between God and man. He was the one who was to hear from God and communicate to mankind a way in which we too could commune directly with God. He came to show us how to live.

The Didache is a manual written from the standpoint of the earliest Jewish messianic sect, called "Christians", for the instruction of converts on how to be Christians and how to conduct themselves in daily life. It is a magnificent view of the beliefs and rituals of the earliest form of Christianity as propagated by those who knew Jesus best; his brother and the original apostles.

The Didache, when placed with the "Q" document, will give the reader a vision of what Christianity was like and what Christians believed during the first twenty to thirty years after the death of Jesus.

The questions before us are these:
Did the original twelve apostles have the full truth, were they incorrect, or has the Christian faith been corrupted? Did the Christian faith evolve into a fuller understanding of God with added beliefs and rituals, or was it subverted and changed into the religion and denominations we have today?
Is the Didache simply history, or is it a way back to the true practice of the faith?

The Didache (Roberts-Donaldson Translation)

The Lord's Teaching Through the Twelve Apostles to the Nations.

Chapter 1.

The Two Ways and the First Commandment. There are two ways, one of life and one of death, but a great difference between the two ways. The way of life, then, is this: First, you shall love God who made you; second, love your neighbor as yourself, and do not do to another what you would not want done to you. And of these sayings the teaching is this: Bless those who curse you, and pray for your enemies, and fast for those who persecute you. For what reward is there for loving those who love you? Do not the Gentiles do the same? But love those who hate you, and you shall not have an enemy. Abstain from fleshly and worldly lusts. If someone strikes your right cheek, turn to him the other also, and you shall be perfect. If someone impresses you for one mile, go with him two. If someone takes your cloak, give him also your coat. If someone takes from you what is yours, ask it not back, for indeed you are not able. Give to every one who asks you, and ask it not back; for the Father wills that to all should be given of our own blessings (free gifts). Happy is he who gives according to the commandment, for he is guiltless. Woe to him who receives; for if one receives who has need, he is guiltless; but he who receives not having need shall pay the penalty, why he received and for what. And coming into confinement, he shall be examined concerning the things which he has done, and he shall not escape from there until he pays back the last penny. And also concerning this, it has been said, Let your alms sweat in your hands, until you know to whom you should give.

Chapter 2.

The Second Commandment: Grave Sin Forbidden. And the second commandment of the Teaching; You shall not commit murder, you shall not commit adultery, you shall not commit pederasty (sexual activity involving a man and a boy), you shall not commit fornication, you shall not steal, you shall not practice magic, you shall not practice witchcraft, you shall not murder a child by abortion nor kill that which is born. You shall not covet the things of your neighbor, you shall not swear, you shall not bear false witness, you shall not speak evil, you shall bear no grudge. You shall not be double-minded nor double-tongued, for to be double-tongued is a snare of death. Your speech shall not be false, nor empty, but fulfilled by deed. You shall not be covetous, nor rapacious, nor a hypocrite, nor evil disposed, nor haughty. You shall not take evil counsel against your neighbor. You shall not hate any man; but some you shall reprove, and concerning some you shall pray, and some you shall love more than your own life.

Chapter 3.

Other Sins Forbidden. My child, flee from every evil thing, and from every likeness of it. Be not prone to anger, for anger leads to murder. Be neither jealous, nor quarrelsome, nor of hot temper, for out of all these murders are engendered. My child, be not a lustful one. for lust leads to fornication. Be neither a filthy talker, nor of lofty eye, for out of all these adulteries are engendered. My child, be not an observer of omens, since it leads to idolatry. Be neither an enchanter, nor an astrologer, nor a purifier, nor be willing to took at these things, for out of all these idolatry is engendered. My child, be not a liar, since a lie leads to theft. Be neither money-loving, nor vainglorious, for out of all these thefts are engendered. My child, be not a murmurer, since it leads the way to blasphemy. Be neither self-willed nor evil-minded, for out of all these blasphemies are engendered.

Rather, be meek, since the meek shall inherit the earth. Be long-suffering and pitiful and guileless and gentle and good and always trembling at the words which you have heard. You shall not exalt yourself, nor give over-confidence to your soul. Your soul shall not be joined with lofty ones, but with just and lowly ones shall it have its intercourse. Accept whatever happens to you as good, knowing that apart from God nothing comes to pass.

Chapter 4.

Various Precepts. My child, remember night and day him who speaks the word of God to you, and honor him as you do the Lord. For wherever the lordly rule is uttered, there is the Lord. And seek out day by day the faces of the saints, in order that you may rest upon their words. Do not long for division, but rather bring those who contend to peace. Judge righteously, and do not respect persons in reproving for transgressions. You shall not be undecided whether or not it shall be. Be not a stretcher forth of the hands to receive and a drawer of them back to give. If you have anything, through your hands you shall give ransom for your sins. Do not hesitate to give, nor complain when you give; for you shall know who is the good repayer of the hire. Do not turn away from him who is in want; rather, share all things with your brother, and do not say that they are your own. For if you are partakers in that which is immortal, how much more in things which are mortal? Do not remove your hand from your son or daughter; rather, teach them the fear of God from their youth. Do not enjoin anything in your bitterness upon your bondman or maidservant, who hope in the same God, lest ever they shall fear not God who is over both; for he comes not to call according to the outward appearance, but to them whom the Spirit has prepared. And you bondmen shall be subject to your masters as to a type of God, in modesty and fear. You shall hate all hypocrisy and everything which is not pleasing to the Lord. Do not in any way forsake the commandments of the Lord; but keep what you have received, neither adding thereto nor taking away therefrom. In the church you shall acknowledge your transgressions, and you shall not come near for your prayer with an evil conscience. This is the way of life.

Chapter 5.

The Way of Death. And the way of death is this: First of all it is evil and accursed: murders, adultery, lust, fornication, thefts, idolatries, magic arts, witchcrafts, rape, false witness, hypocrisy, double-heartedness, deceit, haughtiness, depravity, self-will, greediness, filthy talking, jealousy, over-confidence, loftiness, boastfulness; persecutors of the good, hating truth, loving a lie, not knowing a reward for righteousness, not cleaving to good nor to righteous judgment, watching not for that which is good, but for that which is evil; from whom meekness and endurance are far, loving vanities, pursuing revenge, not pitying a poor man, not laboring for the afflicted, not knowing Him Who made them, murderers of children, destroyers of the handiwork of God, turning away from him who is in want, afflicting him who is distressed, advocates of the rich, lawless judges of the poor, utter sinners. Be delivered, children, from all these.

Chapter 6.

Against False Teachers, and Food Offered to Idols. See that no one causes you to err from this way of the Teaching, since apart from God it teaches you. For if you are able to bear the entire yoke of the Lord, you will be perfect; but if you are not able to do this, do what you are able. And concerning food, bear what you are able; but against that which is sacrificed to idols be exceedingly careful; for it is the service of dead gods.

Chapter 7.

Concerning Baptism. And concerning baptism, baptize this way: Having first said all these things, baptize into the name of the Father, and of the Son, and of the Holy Spirit, in living water. But if you have no living water, baptize into other water; and if you cannot do so in cold water, do so in warm. But if you have neither, pour out water three times upon the head into the name of Father and Son and Holy Spirit. But before the baptism let the baptizer fast, and the baptized, and whoever else can; but you shall order the baptized to fast one or two days before.

Chapter 8.

Fasting and Prayer (the Lord's Prayer). But let not your fasts be with the hypocrites, for they fast on the second and fifth day of the week. Rather, fast on the fourth day and the Preparation (Friday). Do not pray like the hypocrites, but rather as the Lord commanded in His Gospel, like this:

Our Father who art in heaven, hallowed be Thy name. Thy kingdom come. Thy will be done on earth, as it is in heaven. Give us today our daily (needful) bread, and forgive us our debt as we also forgive our debtors. And bring us not into temptation, but deliver us from the evil one (or, evil); for Thine is the power and the glory for ever..

Pray this three times each day.

Chapter 9.

The Eucharist. Now concerning the Eucharist, give thanks this way. First, concerning the cup:

We thank thee, our Father, for the holy vine of David Thy servant, which You madest known to us through Jesus Thy Servant; to Thee be the glory for ever..

And concerning the broken bread:

We thank Thee, our Father, for the life and knowledge which You madest known to us through Jesus Thy Servant; to Thee be the glory for ever. Even as this broken bread was scattered over the hills, and was gathered together and became one, so let Thy Church be gathered together from the ends of the earth into Thy kingdom; for Thine is the glory and the power through Jesus Christ for ever..

But let no one eat or drink of your Eucharist, unless they have been baptized into the name of the Lord; for concerning this also the Lord has said, "Give not that which is holy to the dogs."

Chapter 10.

Prayer after Communion. But after you are filled, give thanks this way:

We thank Thee, holy Father, for Thy holy name which You didst cause to tabernacle in our hearts, and for the knowledge and faith and immortality, which You modest known to us through Jesus Thy Servant; to Thee be the glory for ever. Thou, Master almighty, didst create all things for Thy name's sake; You gavest food and drink to men for enjoyment, that they might give thanks to Thee; but to us You didst freely give spiritual food and drink and life eternal through Thy Servant. Before all things we thank Thee that You are mighty; to Thee be the glory for ever. Remember, Lord, Thy Church, to deliver it from all evil and to make it perfect in Thy love, and gather it from the four winds, sanctified for Thy kingdom which Thou have prepared for it; for Thine is the power and the glory for ever. Let grace come, and let this world pass away. Hosanna to the God (Son) of David! If any one is holy, let him come; if any one is not so, let him repent. Maranatha. Amen.

But permit the prophets to make Thanksgiving as much as they desire.

Chapter 11.

Concerning Teachers, Apostles, and Prophets.
Whosoever, therefore, comes and teaches you all these things that have been said before, receive him. But if the

teacher himself turns and teaches another doctrine to the destruction of this, hear him not. But if he teaches so as to increase righteousness and the knowledge of the Lord, receive him as the Lord. But concerning the apostles and prophets, act according to the decree of the Gospel. Let every apostle who comes to you be received as the Lord. But he shall not remain more than one day; or two days, if there's a need. But if he remains three days, he is a false prophet. And when the apostle goes away, let him take nothing but bread until he lodges. If he asks for money, he is a false prophet. And every prophet who speaks in the Spirit you shall neither try nor judge; for every sin shall be forgiven, but this sin shall not be forgiven. But not every one who speaks in the Spirit is a prophet; but only if he holds the ways of the Lord. Therefore from their ways shall the false prophet and the prophet be known. And every prophet who orders a meal in the Spirit does not eat it, unless he is indeed a false prophet. And every prophet who teaches the truth, but does not do what he teaches, is a false prophet. And every prophet, proved true, working unto the mystery of the Church in the world, yet not teaching others to do what he himself does, shall not be judged among you, for with God he has his judgment; for so did also the ancient prophets. But whoever says in the Spirit, Give me money, or something else, you shall not listen to him. But if he tells you to give for others' sake who are in need, let no one judge him.

Chapter 12.

Reception of Christians. But receive everyone who comes in the name of the Lord, and prove and know him afterward; for you shall have understanding right and left. If he who comes is a wayfarer, assist him as far as you are able; but he shall not remain with you more than two or three days, if need be. But if he wants to stay with you, and is an artisan, let him work and eat. But if he has no trade, according to your understanding, see to it that, as a Christian, he shall not live with you idle. But if he wills not to do, he is a Christ-monger. Watch that you keep away from such.

Chapter 13.

Support of Prophets. But every true prophet who wants to live among you is worthy of his support. So also a true teacher is himself worthy, as the workman, of his support. Every first-fruit, therefore, of the products of wine-press and threshing-floor, of oxen and of sheep, you shall take and give to the prophets, for they are your high priests. But if you have no prophet, give it to the poor. If you make a batch of dough, take the first-fruit and give according to the commandment. So also when you open a jar of wine or of oil, take the first-fruit and give it to the prophets; and of money (silver) and clothing and every possession, take the first-fruit, as it may seem good to you, and give according to the commandment.

Chapter 14.

Christian Assembly on the Lord's Day. But every Lord's day gather yourselves together, and break bread, and give thanksgiving after having confessed your transgressions, that your sacrifice may be pure. But let no one who is at odds with his fellow come together with you, until they be reconciled, that your sacrifice may not be profaned. For this is that which was spoken by the Lord: "In every place and time offer to me a pure sacrifice; for I am a great King, says the Lord, and my name is wonderful among the nations."

Chapter 15.

Bishops and Deacons; Christian Reproof. Appoint, therefore, for yourselves, bishops and deacons worthy of the Lord, men meek, and not lovers of money, and truthful and proved; for they also render to you the service of prophets and teachers. Therefore do not despise them, for they are your honored ones, together with the prophets and teachers. And reprove one another, not in anger, but in peace, as you have it in the Gospel. But to anyone that acts amiss against another, let no one speak, nor let him hear anything from you until he repents. But your prayers and alms and all your deeds so do, as you have it in the Gospel of our Lord.

Chapter 16.

Watchfulness; the Coming of the Lord. Watch for your life's sake. Let not your lamps be quenched, nor your loins unloosed; but be ready, for you know not the hour in which our Lord will come. But come together often, seeking the things which are befitting to your souls: for the whole time of your faith will not profit you, if you are not made perfect in the last time. For in the last days false prophets and corrupters shall be multiplied, and the sheep shall be turned into wolves, and love shall be turned into hate; for when lawlessness increases, they shall hate and persecute and betray one another, and then shall appear the world-deceiver as Son of God, and shall do signs and wonders, and the earth shall be delivered into his hands, and he shall do iniquitous things which have never yet come to pass since the beginning. Then shall the creation of men come into the fire of trial, and many shall be made to stumble and shall perish; but those who endure in their faith shall be saved from under the curse itself. And then shall appear the signs of the truth: first, the sign of an outspreading in heaven, then the sign of the sound of the trumpet. And third, the resurrection of the dead -- yet not of all, but as it is said: "The Lord shall come and all His saints with Him." Then shall the world see the Lord coming upon the clouds of heaven.

Appendix "A"

"That epistle of James gives us much trouble, for the papists embrace it alone and leave out all the rest. Up to this point I have been accustomed just to deal with and interpret it according to the sense of the rest of Scriptures. For you will judge that none of it must be set forth contrary to manifest Holy Scripture.

Accordingly, if they will not admit my interpretations, then I shall make rubble also of it. I almost feel like throwing Jimmy into the stove..." "Therefore St. James' epistle is really an epistle of straw, compared to these others, for it has nothing of the nature of the gospel about it." Martin Luther

THE GENERAL EPISTLE OF JAMES.

CHAPTER 1

JAMES, a servant of God and of the Lord Jesus Christ, to the twelve tribes which are scattered abroad, greeting.

2 My brethren, count it all joy when you fall into divers temptations;

3 Knowing this, that the trying of your faith worketh patience.

4 But let patience have her perfect work, that you may be perfect and entire, wanting nothing.

5 If any of you lack wisdom, let him ask of God, that giveth to all men liberally, and upbraideth not; and it shall be given him.

6 But let him ask in faith, nothing wavering. For he that wavereth is like a wave of the sea driven with the wind and tossed.

7 For let not that man think that he shall receive any thing of the Lord.

8 A double minded man is unstable in all his ways.

9 Let the brother of low degree rejoice in that he is exalted:

10 But the rich, in that he is made low: because as the flower of the grass he shall pass away.

11 For the sun is no sooner risen with a burning heat, but it withereth the grass, and the flower thereof falleth, and the grace of the fashion of it perisheth: so also shall the rich man fade away in his ways.

12 Blessed is the man that endureth temptation: for when he is tried, he shall receive the crown of life, which the Lord has promised to them that love him.

13 Let no man say when he is tempted, I am tempted of God: for God cannot be tempted with evil, neither tempteth he any man:

14 But every man is tempted, when he is drawn away of his own lust, and enticed.

15 Then when lust has conceived, it bringeth forth sin: and sin, when it is finished, bringeth forth death.

16 Do not err, my beloved brethren.

17 Every good gift and every perfect gift is from above, and comes down from the Father of lights, with whom is no variableness, neither shadow of turning.

18 Of his own will begat he us with the word of truth, that we should be a kind of firstfruits of his creatures.

19 Wherefore, my beloved brethren, let every man be swift to hear, slow to speak, slow to wrath:

20 For the wrath of man worketh not the righteousness of God.

21 Wherefore lay apart all filthiness and superfluity of naughtiness, and receive with meekness the engrafted word, which is able to save your souls.

22 But be you doers of the word, and not hearers only, deceiving your own selves.

23 For if any be a hearer of the word, and not a doer, he is like unto a man beholding his natural face in a glass:

24 For he beholdeth himself, and goeth his way, and straightway forgetteth what manner of man he was.

25 But whoso looketh into the perfect law of liberty, and continueth therein, he being not a forgetful hearer, but a doer of the work, this man shall be blessed in his deed.

26 If any man among you seem to be religious, and bridleth not his tongue, but deceiveth his own heart, this man's religion is vain.

27 Pure religion and undefiled before God and the Father is this, To visit the fatherless and widows in their affliction, and to keep himself unspotted from the world.

CHAPTER 2

MY brethren, have not the faith of our Lord Jesus Christ, the Lord of glory, with respect of persons.

2 For if there come unto your assembly a man with a gold ring, in goodly apparel, and there come in also a poor man in vile raiment;

3 And you have respect to him that weareth the gay clothing, and say unto him, Sit you here in a good place; and say to the poor, Stand you there, or sit here under my footstool:

4 Are you not then partial in yourselves, and are become judges of evil thoughts?

5 Hearken, my beloved brethren, Has not God chosen the poor of this world rich in faith, and heirs of the kingdom which he has promised to them that love him?

6 But you have despised the poor. Do not rich men oppress you, and draw you before the judgment seats?

7 Do not they blaspheme that worthy name by the which you are called?

8 If you fulfil the royal law according to the scripture, You

shalt love your neighbour as yourself, you do well:

9 But if you have respect to persons, you commit sin, and are convinced of the law as transgressors.

10 For whosoever shall keep the whole law, and yet offend in one point, he is guilty of all.

11 For he that said, Do not commit adultery, said also, Do not kill. Now if you commit no adultery, yet if you kill, you are become a transgressor of the law.

12 So speak you , and so do, as they that shall be judged by the law of liberty.

13 For he shall have judgment without mercy, that has shewed no mercy; and mercy rejoiceth against judgment.

14 What doth it profit, my brethren, though a man say he has faith, and have not works? can faith save him?

15 If a brother or sister be naked, and destitute of daily food,

16 And one of you say unto them, Depart in peace, be you warmed and filled; notwithstanding you give them not those things which are needful to the body; what doth it profit?

17 Even so faith, if it has not works, is dead, being alone.

18 Yea, a man may say, You have faith, and I have works: shew me your faith without your works, and I will shew you my faith by my works.

19 You believest that there is one God; you doest well: the devils also believe, and tremble.

20 But will you know, O vain man, that faith without works is dead?

21 Was not Abraham our father justified by works, when he had offered Isaac his son upon the altar?

22 Seest you how faith created with his works, and by works was faith made perfect?

23 And the scripture was fulfilled which saith, Abraham believed God, and it was imputed unto him for righteousness: and he was called the Friend of God.

24 You see then how that by works a man is justified, and not by faith only.

25 Likewise also was not Rahab the harlot justified by works, when she had received the messengers, and had sent them out another way?

26 For as the body without the spirit is dead, so faith without works is dead also.

CHAPTER 3

MY brethren, be not many masters, knowing that we shall receive the greater condemnation.

2 For in many things we offend all. If any man offend not in word, the same is a perfect man, and able also to bridle the

whole body.

3 Behold, we put bits in the horses' mouths, that they may obey us; and we turn about their whole body.

4 Behold also the ships, which though they be so great, and are driven of fierce winds, yet are they turned about with a very small helm, whithersoever the governor listeth.

5 Even so the tongue is a little member, and boasteth great things. Behold, how great a matter a little fire kindleth!

6 And the tongue is a fire, a world of iniquity: so is the tongue among our members, that it defileth the whole body, and setteth on fire the course of nature; and it is set on fire of hell.

7 For every kind of beasts, and of birds, and of serpents, and of things in the sea, is tamed, and has been tamed of mankind:

8 But the tongue can no man tame; it is an unruly evil, full of deadly poison.

9 Therewith bless we God, even the Father; and therewith curse we men, which are made after the similitude of God.

10 Out of the same mouth proceedeth blessing and cursing. My brethren, these things ought not so to be.

11 Doth a fountain send forth at the same place sweet water and bitter?

12 Can the fig tree, my brethren, bear olive berries? either a

vine, figs? so can no fountain both yield salt water and fresh.

13 Who is a wise man and endued with knowledge among you? let him shew out of a good conversation his works with meekness of wisdom.

14 But if you have bitter envying and strife in your hearts, glory not, and lie not against the truth.

15 This wisdom descendeth not from above, but is earthly, sensual, devilish.

16 For where envying and strife is, there is confusion and every evil work.

17 But the wisdom that is from above is first pure, then peaceable, gentle, and easy to be intreated, full of mercy and good fruits, without partiality, and without hypocrisy.

18 And the fruit of righteousness is sown in peace of them that make peace.

CHAPTER 4

FROM whence come wars and fightings among you? come they not hence, even of your lusts that war in your members?

2 You lust, and have not: you kill, and desire to have, and cannot obtain: you fight and war, yet you have not, because you ask not.

3 You ask, and receive not, because you ask amiss, that you may consume it upon your lusts.

4 You adulterers and adulteresses, know you not that the friendship of the world is enmity with God? whosoever therefore will be a friend of the world is the enemy of God.

5 Do you think that the scripture saith in vain, The spirit that dwelleth in us lusteth to envy?

6 But he giveth more grace. Wherefore he saith, God resisteth the proud, but giveth grace unto the humble.

7 Submit yourselves therefore to God. Resist the devil, and he will flee from you.

8 Draw nigh to God, and he will draw nigh to you. Cleanse your hands, you sinners; and purify your hearts, you double minded.

9 Be afflicted, and mourn, and weep: let your laughter be turned to mourning, and your joy to heaviness.

10 Humble yourselves in the sight of the Lord, and he shall lift you up.

11 Speak not evil one of another, brethren. He that speaketh evil of his brother, and judgeth his brother, speaketh evil of the law, and judgeth the law: but if you judge the law, you are not a doer of the law, but a judge.

12 There is one lawgiver, who is able to save and to destroy: who are you that judgest another?

13 Go to now, you that say, To day or to morrow we will go into such a city, and continue there a year, and buy and sell, and get gain:

14 Whereas you know not what shall be on the morrow. For what is your life? It is even a vapour, that appeareth for a little time, and then vanisheth away.

15 For that you ought to say, If the Lord will, we shall live, and do this, or that.

16 But now you rejoice in your boastings: all such rejoicing is evil.

17 Therefore to him that knoweth to do good, and doeth it not, to him it is sin.

CHAPTER 5

GO to now, you rich men, weep and howl for your miseries that shall come upon you.

2 Your riches are corrupted, and your garments are motheaten.

3 Your gold and silver is cankered; and the rust of them shall be a witness against you, and shall eat your flesh as it were fire. You have heaped treasure together for the last days.

4 Behold, the hire of the labourers who have reaped down your fields, which is of you kept back by fraud, crieth: and

the cries of them which have reaped are entered into the ears of the Lord of sabaoth.

5 You have lived in pleasure on the earth, and been wanton; you have nourished your hearts, as in a day of slaughter.

6 You have condemned and killed the just; and he doth not resist you.

7 Be patient therefore, brethren, unto the coming of the Lord. Behold, the husbandman waiteth for the precious fruit of the earth, and has long patience for it, until he receive the early and latter rain.

8 Be you also patient; stablish your hearts: for the coming of the Lord draweth nigh.

9 Grudge not one against another, brethren, lest you be condemned: behold, the judge standeth before the door.

10 Take, my brethren, the prophets, who have spoken in the name of the Lord, for an example of suffering affliction, and of patience.

11 Behold, we count them happy which endure. You have heard of the patience of Job, and have seen the end of the Lord; that the Lord is very pitiful, and of tender mercy.

12 But above all things, my brethren, swear not, neither by heaven, neither by the earth, neither by any other oath: but let your yea be yea; and your nay, nay; lest you fall into

condemnation.

13 Is any among you afflicted? let him pray. Is any merry? let him sing psalms.

14 Is any sick among you? let him call for the elders of the church; and let them pray over him, anointing him with oil in the name of the Lord:

15 And the prayer of faith shall save the sick, and the Lord shall raise him up; and if he have committed sins, they shall be forgiven him.

16 Confess your faults one to another, and pray one for another, that you may be healed. The effectual fervent prayer of a righteous man availeth much.

17 Elias was a man subject to like passions as we are, and he prayed earnestly that it might not rain: and it rained not on the earth by the space of three years and six months.

18 And he prayed again, and the heaven gave rain, and the earth brought forth her fruit.

19 Brethren, if any of you do err from the truth, and one convert him;

20 Let him know, that he which converteth the sinner from the error of his way shall save a soul from death, and shall hide a multitude of sins.

Appendix "B"

Didache
Greek Version, Charles Taylor 1889

Διδαχη κυριου δια των δωδεκα αποστολων τοις εθνεσιν.
-1-

1 οδοι δυο εισι, μια της ζωης και μια του θανατου, διαφορα δε πολλη μεταξυ των δυο οδων.

2 η μεν ουν οδος της ζωης εστιν αυτη, πρωτον αγαπησεις τον θεον τον ποιησαντα σε δευτερον τον πλησιον σου ως σεαυτον, παντα δε οσα εαν θελησης μη γινεσθαι σοι, και συ αλλω μη ποιει.

3 τουτων δε των λογων η διδαχη εστιν αυτη, ευλογειτε τους καταρωμενους υμιν και προσευχεσθε υπερ των εχθρων υμων, νηστευετε δε υπερ των διωκοντων υμας, ποια γαρ χαρις, εαν αγαπατε τους αγαπωντας υμας? ουχι και τα εθνη τουτο ποιουσιν, υμεις δε φιλειτε τους μισουντας υμας, και ουχ εξετε εχθρον.

4 απεχου των σαρκικων [και σωματικων] επιθυμιων. εαν τις σοι δω ραπισμα εις την δεξιαν σιαγονα, στρεψον αυτω και την αλλην, και εση τελειος, εαν αγγαρευση σε τις μιλιον εν,

υπαγε μετ' αυτου δυο, εαν αρη τις το ιματιον σου, δος αυτω και τον χιτωνα, εαν λαβη τις απο σου το σον, μη απαιτει, ουδε γαρ δυνασαι.

5 παντι τω αιτουντι σε διδου και μη απαιτει, πασι γαρ θελει διδοσθαι ο πατηρ εκ των ιδιων χαρισματων. μακαριος ο διδους κατα την εντολην, αθωος γαρ εστιν. ουαι τω λαμβανοντι, ει μεν γαρ χρειαν εχων λαμβανει τις, αθωος εσται, ο δε μη χρειαν εχων δωσει δικην, ινατι ελαβε και εις τι, εν συνοχη δε γενομενος εξετασθησεται περι ων επραξε, και ουκ εξελευσεται εκειθεν, μεχρις ου αποδω τον εσχατον κοδραντην.

6 αλλα και περι τουτου δε ειρηται, Ιδρωσατω η ελεημοσυνη σου εις τας χειρας σου, μεχρις αν γνως, τινι δως.

-2-

1 δευτερα δε εντολη της διδαχης,

2 ου φονευσεις, ου μοιχευσεις, ου παιδοφθορησεις, ου πορνευσεις, ου κλεψεις, ου μαγευσεις, ου φαρμακευσεις, ου φονευσεις τεκνον εν φθορα ουδε γεννηθεν αποκτενεις.

3 ουκ επιθυμησεις τα του πλησιον, ουκ επιορκησεις, ου ψευδομαρτυρησεις, ου κακολογησεις, ου μνησικακησεις.

4 ουκ εση διγνωμων ουδε διγλωσσος, παγις γαρ θανατου η διγλωσσια.

5 ουκ εσται ο λογος σου ψευδης, ου κενος, αλλα

μεμεστωμενος πραξει.

6 ουκ εση πλεονεκτης ουδε αρπαξ ουδε υποκριτης ουδε κακοηθης ουδε υπερηφανος. ου ληψη βουλην πονηραν κατα του πλησιον σου

7 ου μισησεις παντα ανθρωπον, αλλα ους μεν ελεγξεις, περι ων δε προσευξη, ους δε αγαπησεις υπερ την ψυχην σου.

-3-

1 τεκνον μου, φευγε απο παντος πονηρου και απο παντος ομοιου αυτου.

2 μη γινου οργιλος, οδηγει γαρ η οργη προς τον φονον, μηδε ζηλωτης μηδε εριστικος μηδε θυμικος, εκ γαρ τουτων απαντων φονοι γεννωνται.

3 τεκνον μου, μη γινου επιθυμητης, οδηγει γαρ η επιθυμια προς την πορνειαν, μηδε αισχρολογος μηδε υψηλοφθαλμος, εκ γαρ τουτων απντων μοιχειαι γεννωνται.

4 τεκνον μου, μη γινου οιωνοσκοπος, επειδη οδηγει εις την ειδωλολατριαν, μηδε επαοιδος μηδε μαθηματικος μηδε περικαθαιρων, μηδε θελε αυτα βλεπειν [μηδε ακουειν], εκ γαρ τουτων απαντων ειδωλολατρια γενναται.

5 τεκνον μου, μη γινου ψευστης, επειδη οδηγει το ψευσμα εις την κλοπην, μηδε φιλαργυρος μηδε κενοδοξος, εκ γαρ τουτων απαντων κλοπαι γεννωνται.

6 τεκνον μου, μη γινου γογγυσος, επειδη οδηγει εις την

βλασφημιαν, μηδε αυθαδης μηδε πονηροφρων, εκ γαρ τουτων απαντων βλασφημιαι γεννωνται.

7 ισθι δε πραυς, επει οι πραεις κληρονομησουσι την γην.

8 γινου μακροθυμος και ελεημων και ακακος και ησυχιος και αγαθος και τρεμων τους λογους δια παντος, ους ηκουσας.

9 ουχ υψωσεις σεαυτον ουδε δωσεις τη ψυχη σου θρασος. ου κολληθησεται η ψυχη σου μετα υφηλων, αλλα μετα δικαιων και ταπεινων αναστραφηση.

10 τα συμβαινοντα σοι ενεργηματα ως αγαθα προσδεξη, ειδως, οτι ατερ θεου ουδεν γινεται.

-4-

1 τεκνον μου, του λαλουντος σοι τον λογον του θεου μνησθηση νυκτος και ημερας, τιμησεις δε αυτον ως κυριον, οθεν γαρ η κυριοτης λαλειται, εκει κυριος εστιν.

2 εκζητησεις δε καθ' ημεραν τα προσωπα των αγιων, ινα επαναπαης τοις λογοις αυτων.

3 ου ποιησεις σχισμα, ειρηνευσεις δε μαχομενους, κρινεις δικαιως, ου ληψη προσωπον ελεγξαι επι παραπτωμασιν.

4 ου διψυχησεις, ποτερον εσται η ου.

5 μη γινου προς μεν το λαβειν εκτεινων τας χειρας, προς δε το δουναι συσπων.

6 εαν εχης δια των χειρων σου, δωσεις λυτρωσιν αμαρτιων

σου.

7 ου διστασεις δουναι ουδε διδους γογγυσεις, γνωση γαρ, τις εστιν ο του μισθου καλος ανταποδοτης.

8 ουκ αποστραφηση τον ενδεομενον, συγκοινωνησεις δε παντα τω αδελφω σου και ουκ ερεις ιδια ειναι, ει γαρ εν τω αθανατω κοινωνοι εστε, ποσω μαλλον εν τοις θνητοις?

9 ουκ αρεις την χειρα σου απο του υιου σου η απο της θυγατρος σου, αλλα απο νεοτητος διδαξεις τον φοβον του θεου.

10 ουκ επιταξεις δουλω σου η παιδισκη, τοις επι τον αυτον θεον ελπιζουσιν, εν πικρια σου, μηποτε ου μη φοβηθησονται τον επ' αμφοτεροις θεον, ου γαρ ερχεται κατα προσωπον καλεσαι, αλλ' εφ' ους το πνευμα ητοιμασεν.

11 υμεις δε [οι] δουλοι υποταγησεσθε τοις κυριοις υμων ως τυπω θεου εν αισχυνη και φοβω.

12 μισησεις πασαν υποκρισιν και παν ο μη αρεστον τω κυριω.

13 ου μη εγκαταλιπης εντολας κυριου, φυλαξεις δε α παρελαβες, μητε προστιθεις μητε αφαιρων.

14 εν εκκλεσια εξομολογηση τα παραπτωματα σου, και ου προσελευση επι προσευχην σου εν συνειδησει πονηρα. αυτη εστιν η οδος της ζωης.

-5-

1 η δε του θανατου οδος εστιν αυτη, πρωτον παντων πονηρα εστι και καταρας μεστη, φονοι, μοιχειαι, επιθυμιαι, πορνειαι, κλοπαι, ειδωλολατριαι, μαγειαι, φαρμακιαι, αρπαγαι, ψευδομαρτυριαι, υποκρισεις, διπλοκαρδια, δολος, υπερηφανια, κακια, αυθαδεια, πλεονεξια, αισχρολογια, ζηλοτυπια, θρασυτης, υψος, αλαζονεια, [αφοβια].

2 διωκται αγαθων, μισουντες αληθειαν, αγαπωντες ψευδος, ου γινωσκοντες μισθον δικαιοσυνης, ου κολλωμενοι αγαθω ουδε κρισει δικαια, αγρυπνουντες ουκ εις το αγαθον, αλλ' εις το πονηρον, ων μακραν πραυτης και υπομονη, ματαια αγαπωντες, διωκοντες ανταποδομα, ουκ ελεουντες πτωχον, ου πονουντες επι καταπονουμενω, ου γινωσκοντες τον ποιησαντα αυτους, φονεις τεκνων, φθορεις πλασματος θεου, αποστρεφομενοι τον ενδεομενον, καταπονουντες τον θλιβομενον, πλουσιων παρακλητοι, πενητων ανομοι κριται, πανθαμαρτητοι, ρυσθειητε, τεκνα, απο τουτων απαντων.

-6-

1 ορα, μη τις σε πλανηση απο ταυτης της οδου της διδαχης, επει παρεκτος θεου σε διδασκει.

2 ει μεν γαρ δυνασαι βαστασαι ολον τον ζυγον του κυριου, τελειος εση, ει δ' ου δυνασαι, ο δυνη, τουτο ποιει.

3 περι δε της βρωσεως, ο δυνασαι βαστασον, απο δε του ειδωλοθυτου λιαν προσεχε, λατρεια γαρ εστι θεων νεκρων.

-7-

1 περι δε του βαπτισματος, ουτω βαπτισατε, ταυτα παντα προειποντες, βαπτισατε εις το ονομα του πατρος και του υιου και του αγιου πνευματος εν υδατι ζωντι.

2 εαν δε μη εχης υδωρ ζων, εις αλλο υδωρ βαπτισον, ει δ' ου δυνασαι εν ψυχρω, εν θερμω.

3 εαν δε αμφοτερα μη εχης, εκχεον εις την κεφαλην τρις υδωρ εις ονομα πατρος και υιου και αγιου πνευματος.

4 προ δε του βαπτισματος προνηστευσατω ο βαπτιζων και ο βαπτιζομενος και ει τινες αλλοι δυνανται, κελευεις δε νηστευσαι τον βαπτιζομενον προ μιας η δυο.

-8-

1 αι δε νηστειαι υμων μη εστωσαν μετα των υποκριτων. νηστευσουσι γαρ δευτερα σαββατων και πεμπτη, υμεις δε νηστευσατε τετραδα και παρασκευην.

2 μηδε προσευχεσθε ως οι υποκριται, αλλ' ως εκελευσεν ο κυριος εν τω ευαγγελιω αυτου, ουτω προσευχεσθε, πατηρ ημων ο εν τω ουρανω, αγιασθητω το ονομα σου, ελθετω η βασιλεια σου, γενηθητω το θελημα σου ως εν ουρανω και επι γης, τον αρτον ημων τον επιουσιον δος ημιν σημερον, και αφες ημιν την οφειλην ημων, ως και ημεις αφιεμεν τοις οφειλεταις ημων, και μη εισενεγκης ημας εις πειρασμον,

αλλα ρυσαι ημας απο του πονηρου, οτι σου εστιν η δυναμις και η δοξα εις τους αιωνας.

3 τρις της ημερας ουτω προσευχεσθε.

-9-

1 περι δε της ευχαριστιας, ουτως ευχαριστησατε,

2 πρωτον περι του ποτηριου, ευχαριστουμεν σοι, πατερ ημων, υπερ της αγιας αμπελου δαυιδ του παιδος σου, ης εγνωρισας ημιν δια Ιησου του παιδος σου, σοι η δοξα εις τους αιωνας.

3 περι δε του κλασματος, ευχαριστουμεν σοι, πατερ ημων, υπερ της ζωης και γνωσεως, ης εγνωρισας ημιν δια Ιησου του παιδος σου. σοι η δοξα εις τους αιωνας.

4 ωσπερ ην τουτο [το] κλασμα διεσκορπισμενον επανω των ορεων και συναχθεν εγενετο εν, ουτω συναχθητω σου η εκκλησια απο των περατων της γης εις την σην βασιλειαν, οτι σου εστιν η δοξα και η δυναμις δια Ιησου Cριστου εις τους αιωνας.

5 μηδεις δε φαγετω μηδε πιετω απο της ευχαριστιας υμων, αλλ' οι βαπτισθεντες εις ονομα κυριου, και γαρ περι τουτου ειρηκεν ο κυριος. μη δωτε το αγιον τοις κυσι.

-10-

1 μετα δε το εμπλησθηναι ουτως ευχαριστησατε,

2 ευχαριστουμεν σοι, πατερ αγιε, υπερ του αγιου ονοματος σου, ου κατεσκηνωσας εν ταις καρδιαις ημων, και υπερ της γνωσεως και πιστεως και αθανασιας, ης εγνωρισας ημιν δια Ιησου του παιδος σου, σοι η δοξα εις τους αιωνας.

3 συ, δεσποτα παντοκρατορ, εκτισας τα παντα ενεκεν του ονοματος σου, τροφην τε και ποτον εδωκας τοις ανθρωποις εις απολαυσιν, ινα σοι ευχαριστησωσιν, ημιν δε εχαρισω πνευματικην τροφην και ποτον και ζωην αιωνιον δια Ιησου του παιδος σου.

4 προ παντων ευχαριστουμεν σοι, οτι δυνατος ει, σοι η δοξα εις τους αιωνας.

5 μνησθητι, κυριε, της εκκλησιας σου του ρυσασθαι αυτην απο παντος πονηρου και τελειωσαι αυτην εν τη αγαπη σου, και συναξον αυτην απο των τεσσαρων ανεμων, την αγιασθεισαν, εις την σην βασιλειαν, ην ητοιμασας αυτη, οτι σου εστιν η δυναμις και η δοξα εις τους αιωνας.

6 ελθετω χαρις και παρελθετω ο κοσμος ουτος. ωσαννα τω θεω δαυιδ. ει τις αγιος εστιν, ερχεσθω, ει τις ουκ εστι, μετανοειτω, μαραν αθα, αμην.

7 τοις δε προφηταις επιτρεπετε ευχαριστειν, οσα θελουσιν.

-10β-

1 [περι δε του μυρου ουτως ευχαριστησατε,

2 ευχαριστουμεν σοι, πατερ ημων αγιε, υπερ του μυρου, ου

εγνωρισας ημιν δια Ιησου του παιδος σου, σοι η δοξα εις τους αιωνας, αμην]

-11-

1 ος αν ουν ελθων διδαξη υμας ταυτα παντα τα προειρημενα, δεξασθε αυτον,

2 εαν δε αυτος ο διδασκων στραφεις διδασκη αλλην διδαχην εις το καταλυσαι, μη αυτου ακουσητε, εις δε το προςθειναι δικαιοσυνην και γνωσιν κυριου, δεξασθε αυτον ως κυριον.

3 περι δε των αποστολων και προφητων, κατα το δογμα του ευαγγελιου ουτω ποιησατε.

4 πας δε αποστολος ερχομενος προς υμας.

5 ου μενει [ει μη] ημεραν μιαν, εαν δε η χρεια, και την αλλην, τρεις δε εαν μεινη, ψευδοπροφητης εστιν.

6 εξερχομενος δε ο αποστολος μηδεν λαμβανετω ει μη αρτον, εως ου αυλισθη, εαν δε αργυριον αιτη, ψευδοπροφητης εστι.

7 και παντα προφητην λαλουντα εν πνευματι ου πειρασετε ουδε διακρινειτε, πασα γαρ αμαρτια αφεθησεται, αυτη δε η αμαρτια ουκ αφεθησεται.

8 ου πας δε ο λαλων εν πνευματι προφητης εστιν, αλλ' εαν εχη τους τροπους κυριου. απο ουν των τροπων γνωσθησεται ο ψευδοπροφητης και ο προφητης.

9 και πας προφητης οριζων τραπεζαν εν πνευματι, ου φαγεται απ' αυτης, ει δε μηγε ψευδοπροφητης εστι.

10 πας δε προφητης διδασκων την αληθειαν, ει α διδασκει ου ποιει, ψευδοπροφητης εστι.

11 πας δε προφητης δεδοκιμασμενος, αληθινος, ποιων εις μυστηριον κοσμικον εκκλησιας, μη διδασκων δε ποιειν, οσα αυτος ποιει, ου κριθησεται εφ' υμων, μετα θεου γαρ εχει την κρισιν, ωσαυτως γαρ εποιησαν και οι αρχαιοι προφηται.

12 ος δ' αν ειπη εν πνευματι, δος μοι αργυρια η ετερα τινα, ουκ ακουσεσθε αυτου, εαν δε περι αλλων υστερουντων ειπη δουναι, μηδεις αυτον κρινετω.

-12-

1 πας δε ο ερχομενος προς υμας εν ονοματι κυριου δεχθητω, επειτα δε δοκιμασαντες αυτον γνωσεσθε, συνεσιν γαρ εχετε δεξιαν και αριστεραν.

2 ει μεν παροδιος εστιν ο ερχομενος, βοηθειτε αυτω, οσον δυνασθε, ου μενει δε προς υμας ει μη δυο η τρεις ημερας, εαν η αναγκη.

3 ει δε θελει προς υμας καθησθαι, τεχνιτης ων, εργαζεσθω και φαγετω.

4 ει δε ουκ εχει τεχνην, κατα την συνεσιν υμων προνοησατε, πως μη αργος μεθ' υμων ζησεται Cριστιανος.

5 ει δ' ου θελει ουτω ποιειν, χριστεμπορος εστι, προσεχετε απο των τοιουτων.

-13-

1 πας δε προφητης αληθινος, θελων καθησθαι προς υμας, αξιος εστι της τροφης αυτου.

2 ωσαυτως διδακαλος αληθινος εστιν αξιος και αυτος ωσπερ ο εργατης της τροφης αυτου.

3 πασαν ουν απαρχην γεννηματων ληνου και αλωνος, βοων τε και προβατων λαβων δωσεις την απαρχην τοις προφηταις, αυτοι γαρ εισιν οι αρχιερεις υμων.

4 εαν δε μη εχητε προφητην, δοτε τοις πτωχοις.

5 εαν σιτιαν ποιης, την απαρχην λαβων δος κατα την εντολην.

6 ωσαυτως κεραμιον οινου η ελαιου ανοιξας, την απαρχην λαβων δος τοις προφηταις,

7 αργυριου δε και ιματισμου και παντος κτηματος λαβων την απαρχην ως αν σοι δοξη, δος κατα την εντολην.

-14-

1 κατα κυριακην δε κυριου συναχθεντες κλασατε αρτον και ευχαριστησατε, προεξομολογησαμενοι τα παραπτωματα υμων, οπως καθαρα η θυσια υμων η.

2 πας δε εχων την αμφιβολιαν μετα του εταιρου αυτου μη

συνελθετω υμιν, εως ου διαλλαγωσιν, ινα μη κοινωθη η θυσια υμων.

3 αυτη γαρ εστιν η ρηθεισα υπο κυριου, εν παντι τοπω και χρονω προσφερειν μοι θυσιαν καθαραν, οτι βασιλευς μεγας ειμι, λεγει κυριος, και το ονομα μου θαυμαστον εν τοις εθνεσι.

-15-

1 χειροτονησατε ουν εαυτοις επισκοπους και διακονους αξιους του κυριου, ανδρας πραεις και αφιλαργυρους και αληθεις και δεδοκιμασμενους, υμιν γαρ λειτουργουσι και αυτοι την λειτουργιαν των προφητων και διδασκαλων.

2 μη ουν υπεριδητε αυτους, αυτοι γαρ εισιν οι τετιμημενοι υμων μετα των προφητων και διδασκαλων.

3 ελεγχετε δε αλληλους μη εν οργη, αλλ' εν ειρηνη ως εχετε εν τω ευαγγελιω, και παντι αστοχουντι κατα του ετερου μηδεις λαλειτω μηδε παρ' υμων ακουετω, εως ου μετανοηση.

4 τας δε ευχας υμων και τας ελεημοσυνας και πασας τας πραξεις ουτω ποιησατε, ως εχετε εν τω ευαγγελιω του κυριου ημων.

-16-

1 γρηγορειτε υπερ της ζωης υμων, οι λυχνοι υμων μη

σβεσθητωσαν, και αι οσφυες υμων μη εκλυεσθωσαν, αλλα γινεσθε ετοιμοι, ου γαρ οιδατε την ωραν, εν η ο κυριος ημων ερχεται.

2 πυκνως δε συναχθησεσθε ζητουντες τα ανηκοντα ταις ψυχαις υμων, ου γαρ ωφελησει υμας ο πας χρονος της πιστεως υμων, εαν μη εν τω εσχατω καιρω τελειωθητε.

3 εν γαρ ταις εσχαταις ημεραις πληθυνθησονται οι ψευδοπροφηται και οι φθορεις, και στραφησονται τα προβατα εις λυκους, και η αγαπη στραφησεται εις μισος.

4 αυξανουσης γαρ της ανομιας μισησουσιν αλληλους και παραδωσουσι, και τοτε φανησεται ο κοσμοπλανης ως υιος θεου και ποιησει σημεια και τερατα, και η γη παραδοθησεται εις χειρας αυτου, και ποιησει αθεμιτα, α ουδεποτε γεγονεν εξ αιωνος.

5 τοτε ηξει η κτισις των ανθρωπων εις την πυρωσιν της δοκιμασιας, και σκανδαλισθησονται πολλοι και απολουνται, οι δε υπομειναντες εν τη πιστει αυτων σωθησονται υπ' αυτου του καταθεματος.

6 και τοτε φανησεται τα σημεια της αληθειας, πρωτον σημειον εκπετασεως εν ουρανω, ειτα σημειον φωνης σαλπιγγος, και το τριτον αναστασις νεκρων,

7 ου παντων δε, αλλ' ως ερρεθη, ηξει ο κυριος και παντες οι αγιοι μετ' αυτου.

8 τοτε οψεται ο κοσμος τον κυριον ερχομενον επανω των

νεφελων του ουρανου.

Appendix "C"

The "Q" Source Based on Luke.

"Q" is an abbreviation for Quelle, the German word for "source." The prevailing theory in the study of the gospels of Matthew, Mark and Luke is that Mark was the first gospel, Matthew and Luke are rewritten versions of Mark. But there are very many sayings in Matthew and in Luke that are NOT in Mark.

These, it is thought, came from a common written source (or Quelle) that is now known as "Q". Often Q sayings are word-for-word the same in Greek in both Matthew and Luke and often are in the same order. This means to most scholars that Q was a written text (no longer in existence) and not simply oral tradition. Many Q sayings are also to be found in the Gospel of Thomas. Thomas is NOT Q but Thomas is a list of saying, like "Q", which in many ways runs parallel to the sayings of "Q".

3:7-9 [John the Baptist] said to the multitudes that came out to be baptized by him, "You brood of vipers! Who warned you to flee from the wrath to come? Bear fruits that befit repentance, and do not begin to say to yourselves, we have Abraham as our father'; for I tell you, God is able from these stones to raise up children to Abraham. Even now the axe is laid to the root of the trees; every tree therefore that does not bear good fruit is cut down and thrown into the fire."

3:16-17 John answered them all, "I baptize you with water; but he who is mightier than I is coming, the thong of whose sandals I am not worthy to untie; he will baptize you with the Holy Spirit and with fire. His winnowing fork is in his hand, to clear his threshing floor, and to gather the wheat into his granary, but the chaff he will burn with unquenchable fire."

4:1-13 Jesus, full of the Holy spirit, returned from the Jordan and was led by the Spirit for forty days in the wilderness, tempted by the devil. He ate nothing in those days; and when they were ended, he was hungry.

The devil said to him, "If you are the Son of God, command this stone to become bread." Jesus answered him, "It is written, 'Man shall not live by bread alone." The devil took him up, and showed him all the kingdoms of the world in a moment of time, and said to him, "To you I will give all this authority and their glory; for it has been delivered to me, and I give it to whom I will, if you, then, will worship me, it shall all be yours." And Jesus answered him, 'It is written, 'you shall worship the Lord your God, and him only shall you serve.'" He took him to Jerusalem and set him on the pinnacle of the temple and said to him 'If you are the Son of God throw yourself down from here; for it is written, 'He will give his angels charge of you, to guard you, and on their hands they will bear you up, lest you strike your foot against a stone.' " Jesus answered him, "It is said, 'you shall not tempt the Lord your God.' "And when the devil had ended every temptation, he departed from him until an opportune time.

6:20b-21 Blessed are you poor, for yours is the kingdom of God. Blessed are you that hunger now, for you shall be satisfied. Blessed are you that weep now, for you shall laugh.

6:22-23 Blessed are you when men hate you, and when they exclude you and revile you, and cast out your name as evil, on account of the Son of man! Rejoice in that day, and leap for joy, for behold, your reward is great in heaven; for so their fathers did to the prophets.

6:27-28 But I say to you that hear, Love your enemies, do good to those who hate you, bless those who curse you, pray for those who abuse you.

6:29 To him who strikes you on the cheek, offer the other also; and from him who takes away your cloak do not withhold your coat as well.

6:30 Give to every one who begs from you; and of him who takes away your goods do not ask them again.

6:31 As you wish that men would do to you, do so to them.

6:32-35 If you love those who love you, what credit is that to you? For even sinners love those who love them. If you do good to those who do good to you, what credit is that to you? For even sinners do the same. If you lend to those from whom you hope to receive what credit is that to you? Even sinners lend to sinners, to receive as much again. But love your enemies, and do good, and lend, expecting nothing in return; and your reward will be great, and you will be sons of the Most High; for he is kind to the ungrateful and the selfish.

6:36 Be merciful, even as your Father is merciful.

6:37-38 Judge not, and you will not be judged; condemn not, and you will not be condemned; forgive, and you will be forgiven; and give and it will be given to you; good measure, pressed down, shaken together, running over, will be put into your lap. For the measure you give will be the measure you get back."

6:39 Can a blind man lead a blind man? Will they not both fall into a pit?

6:40 A disciple is not above his teacher, but every one when he is fully taught will be like his teacher.

6:41-42 Why do you see the speck that is in your brother's eye, but do not notice the log that is in your own eye? Or how can you say to your brother,

'Brother, let me take out the speck that is in your eye,' when you yourself do not see the log that is in your own eye? You hypocrite, first take the log out of your own eye, and then you will see clearly to take out the speck that is in your brother's eye.

6:43-44 For no good tree bears bad fruit, nor again does a bad tree bear good fruit; 44 for each tree is known by its own fruit, For figs are not gathered from thorns, nor are grapes picked from a bramble bush.

6:45 The good man out of the good treasure of his heart produces good, and the evil man out of his evil treasure produces evil; for out of the abundance of the heart his mouth speaks.

6:46 Why do you call me 'Lord, Lord,' and not do what I tell you?

6:47-49 Every one who comes to me and hears my words and does them, I will show you what he is like: he is like a man building a house, who dug deep, and built the foundation upon rock; and when a flood arose, the stream broke against that house, and could not shake it, because it had been well built. But he who hears and does not do them is like a man who built a house on the ground without a foundation, against which the stream broke, and immediately it fell, and the ruin of that house was great.

7:1-10 A centurion had a slave who was dear to him who was sick and at the point of death. When he heard of Jesus he sent to him elders of the Jews, asking him to come and heal his slave. When they came to Jesus they besought him earnestly, saying, "He is worthy to have you do this for him, for he loves our nation, and he built us our synagogue." Jesus went with them. When he was not far from the house, the centurion sent friends to him, saying to him, Lord do not trouble yourself, for I am not worthy to have you come under my roof; therefore I did not presume to come to you. But say the word, and let my servant be healed. For I am a man set under authority, with soldiers under me: and I say to one, 'Go,' and he goes; and to another, 'come,' and he comes; and to my slave, 'Do this,' and he does it," when Jesus heard this he marveled at him, and turned and said to the multitude that followed him, 'I tell you, not even in Israel have I found such faith."

When those who had been sent returned to the house, they found the slave well.

7:18-23 The disciples of John told him all these things. John calling to him two of his disciples, sent them to the Lord, saying, 'Are you he who is to come, or shall we look or another?" When the men had come to him, they said, John the Baptist has sent us to you, saying, Are you he who is to come or shall we look for another?' In that hour he cured many of diseases and plagues and evil spirits, and on many that were blind he bestowed sight. He answered them, "Go and tell John what you have seen and heard; the blind receive their sight, the lame walk, lepers are cleansed, and the deaf hear, the dead are raised up, the poor have good news preached to them, and blessed is he who takes no offense at me."

7:24-26 When the messengers of John had gone, he began to speak to the crowds concerning John: What did you go out into the wilderness to behold? A reed shaken by the wind? What then did you go out to see? A man clothed in soft raiment? Behold, those who are gorgeously appareled and live in luxury are in kings' courts. What then did you go out to see? A prophet? Yes, I tell you, and more than a prophet.

7:27 This is he of whom it is written, Behold, I send my messenger before thy face, who shall prepare thy way before thee.

7:28 I tell you, among those born of women none is greater than John; yet he who is least in the kingdom of God is greater than he.

7:31-34 To what shall I compare the men of this generation, and what are they like? They are like children sitting in the market place and calling to one another, We piped to you, and you did not dance; we wailed, and you did not weep. John the Baptist has come eating no bread and drinking no wine; and you say, He has a demon.' The Son of man has come eating and drinking; and you say, Behold, a glutton and a drunkard, a friend of tax collectors and sinners!'

7:35 Wisdom is justified by all her children."

9:57-58 Foxes have holes, and birds of the air have nests; but the son of man has nowhere to lay his head.

9:59-60 To another he said, Follow me." But he said, "Lord, let me first go and bury my father." But he said to him, leave the dead to bury their own dead; but as for you, go and proclaim the kingdom of God."

10:2 He said to them, The harvest is plentiful, but the laborers are few; pray therefore the Lord of the harvest to send out laborers into his harvest.

10:3 Go your way; behold, I send you out as lambs in the midst of wolves. Carry no purse, no bag, no sandals; salute no one on the road. Whatever house you enter, first say, 'Peace be to this house!' And if a son of peace is there, your peace shall rest upon him; but if not, it shall return to you.

10:7 Remain in the same house, eating and drinking what they provide, for the laborer deserves his wages. Do not go from house to house.

10:8-9 Whenever you enter a town and they receive you, eat what is set before you; heal the sick in it and say to them, 'The kingdom of God has come near to you.

10:10-11 Whenever you enter a town and they do not receive you, go into its streets and say: 'Even the dust of your town that clings to our feet, we wipe off against you; nevertheless know this, that the kingdom of God has come near.'

10:12 I tell you, it shall be more tolerable on that day for Sodom than for that town.

10:13-15 Woe to you, Chorazin! woe to you, Bethsaida! for if the mighty works done in you had been done in Tyre and Sidon, they would have repented long ago, sitting in sackcloth and ashes. But it shall be more tolerable in the judgement for Tyre and Sidon than for you. And you, Capernaum, will you be exalted to heaven? You shall be brought down to Hades.

10:16 He who hears you hears me, and he who rejects you rejects me, and he who rejects me rejects him who sent me.

10:21-22 He rejoiced in the Holy Spirit and said, 'I thank thee, Father, Lord of heaven and earth, that thou hast hidden these things from the wise and understanding and revealed them to babes; yea, Father, for such was thy gracious will. All things have been delivered to me by my Father; and no one knows who the Son is except the Father, or who the Father is except the Son and any one to whom the Son chooses to reveal him.'

10:23-24 Blessed are the eyes which see what you see! For I tell you that many prophets and kings desired to see what you see, and did not see it, and to hear what you hear, and did not hear it.

11:2-4 When you pray, say, 'Father, hallowed be thy name, Thy kingdom come. Give us each day our daily bread; and forgive us our sins, for we ourselves forgive every one who is indebted to us; and lead us not into temptation.'

11:9-10 Ask, and it will be given you; seek, and you will find; knock, and it will be opened to you. Everyone who asks receives, and he who seeks finds, and to him who knocks it will be opened.

11:11-13 What father among you, if his son asks for a fish, will instead of a fish give him a serpent; 12 or if he asks for an egg, will give him a scorpion? If you then, who are evil, know how to give good gifts to your children, how much more will the heavenly Father give the Holy Spirit to those who ask him!

11:14-15 He was casting out a demon that was dumb; when the demon had gone out, the dumb man spoke, and the people marveled. But some of them said, "He casts out demons by Beelzebub, the prince of demons"

11:17-18 "Every kingdom divided against itself is laid waste, and house falls upon house. If Satan also is divided against himself, how can his kingdom stand?

11:19 For you say that I cast out demons by Beelzebub. If I cast out demons by Beelzebub, by whom do your sons cast them out? Therefore they shall be your judges.

11:20 If it is by the finger of God that I cast out demons, then the kingdom of God has come upon you.

11:21-22 When a strong man, fully armed, guards his own palace, his good are in peace; but when one stronger than he assails him and overcomes him, he takes away his armor in which he trusted and divides his spoil.

11:23 He who is not with me is against me, and he who does not gather with me scatters.

11:24-26 When the unclean spirit has gone out of a man, he passes through waterless places seeking rest; and finding none he says, I will return to my house from which I came.' When he comes he finds it swept and put in order. Then he goes and brings seven spirits more evil than himself, and they enter and dwell there; and the last state of that man becomes worse than the first.

11:29 This generation is an evil generation; it seeks a sign, but no sign shall be given to it except the sign of Jonah.

11:30 As Jonah became a sign to the men of Nineveh, so will the Son of man be to this generation.

11:31-32 The queen of the South will arise at the judgment with the men of this generation and condemn them; for she came from the ends of the earth to hear the wisdom of Solomon, and behold, something greater than Solomon is here. The men of Nineveh will arise at the judgment with this generation and condemn it; for they repented at the preaching of Jonah, and behold, something greater than Jonah is here.

11:33 No one after lighting a lamp puts it in a cellar or under a bush, but on a stand, that those who enter may see the light.

11:34-36 Your eye is the lamp of your body; when your eye is sound, your whole body is full of light; but when it is not sound, your body is full of darkness. Therefore be careful lest the light in you be darkness. If then your whole body is full of light, having no part dark, it will be wholly bright, as when a lamp with its rays gives you light.

11:39-41 You Pharisees cleanse the outside of the cup and of the dish, but inside you are full of extortion and wickedness. to You fools! Did not he who made the outside make the inside also? But give for alms those things which are within and behold, everything is clean for you.

11:42 Woe to you Pharisees! for you tithe mint and rue and every herb, and neglect justice and the love of God; these you ought to have done, without neglecting the others.

11:43 Woe to you Pharisees! for you love the best seat in the synagogues and salutations in the Market places.

11:44 Woe to you! for you are like graves which are not seen, and men walk over them without knowing it."

11:46 Woe to you lawyers also! for you load men with burdens hard to bear, and you yourselves do not touch the burdens with one of your fingers.

11:47-48 Woe to you for you build the tombs of the prophets whom your fathers killed. So you are witnesses and consent to the deeds of your fathers; they killed them, and you build their tombs. 11:49-51 The Wisdom of God said, "I will send them prophets and apostles, some of whom they will kill and persecute,' that the blood of all the prophets, shed from the foundation of the world may be required of this generation, from the blood of Abel to the blood of Zechariah, who perished between the altar and the sanctuary. Yes, I tell you, it shall be required of this generation.

11:52 Woe to you lawyers! for you have taken away the key of knowledge; you did not enter yourselves and you hindered those who were entering.

12:2 Nothing is covered up that will not be revealed, or hidden that will not be known.

12:3 Whatever you have said in the dark shall be heard in the light, and what you have whispered in private rooms shall be proclaimed upon the housetops.

12:4-5 I tell you, my friends, do not fear those who kill the body, and after that have no more that they can do. But I will warn you whom to fear: fear him who, after he has killed, has power to cast into hell; yes, I tell you fear him!

12:6-7 Are not five sparrows sold for two pennies? And not one of them is forgotten before God. Why even the hairs of your head are all numbered. Fear not; you are of more value than many sparrows.

12:8-9 I tell you, every one who acknowledges me before men, the Son of man also will acknowledge before the angels of God; but he who denies me before men will be denied before the angels of God.

12:10 Every one who speaks a word against the Son of man will be forgiven; but he who blasphemes against the Holy Spirit will not be forgiven.

12:11-12 When they bring you before the synagogues and the rulers and the authorities, do not be anxious how or what you are to answer or what you are to say; for the Holy Spirit will teach you in that very hour what you ought to say.

12:22 Do not be anxious about your life, what you shall eat nor about your body, what you shall put on.

12:23 Life is more than food, and the body more than clothing.

12:24 Consider the ravens, they neither sow nor reap. they have

neither storehouse nor barn, and yet God feeds them. Of how much more value are you than the birds !

12:25-26 Which of you by being anxious can add a cubit to his span of life? If then you are not able to do as small a thing as that, why are you anxious about the rest?

12:27 Consider the lilies, how they grow; they neither toil nor spin; yet I tell you, even Solomon in all his glory was not arrayed like one of these.

12:28 But if God so clothes the grass which is alive in the field today and tomorrow is thrown into the oven, how much more will he clothe you, O men of little faith!

12:29-30 Do not seek what you are to eat and what you are to drink, nor be of anxious mind. For all the nations of the world seek these things; and your Father knows that you need them. Instead seek his kingdom, and these things shall be yours as well.

12:33-34 Sell your possessions, and give alms; provide your selves with purses that do not grow old, with a treasure in the heavens that does not fail, where no thief approaches and no moth destroys. For where your treasure is, there will your heart be also.

12:39-40 If the householder had known at what hour the thief was coming, he would have been awake and would not have let his house to be broken into, you also must be ready; for the Son of man is coming at an hour you do not expect.

12:42-46 The Lord said, 'Who then is the faithful and wise steward, whom his master will set over his household, to give them their portion of food at the proper time? Blessed is that servant whom his master when he comes will find so doing. Truly I tell you, he will set him over all his possessions. But if that servant says to himself, 'My master is delayed in coming,' and begins to beat the menservants and the maidservants, and to eat and drink and get drunk, the master of that servant will come on a day when he does not expect him and at an hour he does not know, and will punish him, and put him with the unfaithful.

12:49 I came to cast fire upon the earth; and would that it were already kindled!

12:52-53 Do you think that I have come to give peace on earth? No, I tell you, but rather division; 52 for henceforth in one house there will be five divided, three against two and two against three; they will be divided, father against son and son against father, mother against daughter and daughter against her mother, mother-in-law against her daughter-in-law and daughter-in-law against her mother-in-law.

12:57-59 Why do you not judge for yourselves what is right? As you go with your accuser before the magistrate, make an effort to settle with him on the way, lest he drag you to the judge, and the judge hand you over to the officer, and the officer put you in prison. I tell you, you will never get out till you have paid the very last copper.

13:18-19 He said, "What is the kingdom of God like? To what shall I compare it?" It is like a grain of mustard seed which a man took, and sowed in his garden; and it grew and became a tree, and the birds of the air made nests in its branches."

13:20-21 He said, "To what shall I compare the kingdom of God? 21 It is like leaven which a woman took and hid in three measures of meal, till it was all leavened."

13:24 Strive to enter by the narrow door; for many, I tell you, will seek to enter and will not be able.

13:25-27 When once the householder has risen up and shut the door, you will begin to stand outside and to knock at the door, saying, 'Lord, open to us.' He will answer you, 'I do not know where you come from,' Then you will begin to say, we ate and drank in your presence, and you taught in our streets.' But he will say, 'I tell you, I do not know where you come from; depart from me, all you workers of iniquity!'

13:28-29 You will weep and gnash your teeth, when you see Abraham and Isaac and Jacob and all the prophets in the kingdom of God and you yourselves thrust out. Men will come from east and west, and from north and south, and sit at table in the kingdom of God.

13:30 Some are last who will be first, and some are first who will be last.

13:34-35 0 Jerusalem, Jerusalem! How often would I have gathered your children together as a hen gathers her brood under her wings, and you would not! Behold, your house is forsaken. I tell you, you will not see me until you say, Blessed is he who comes in the name of the Lord!"

14:16-24 A man once gave a great banquet, and invited many and at the time of the banquet he sent his servant to say to those who had been invited, 'Come for all is now ready.' But they all alike began to make excuses. The first said to him, 'I have bought a field, and I must go out and see it; I pray you, have me excused.' 19 And another said, 'I have bought a yoke of oxen, I pray you, have me excused,' And another said, 'I have married a wife, and therefore I cannot come.' So the servant came and reported this to his master. Then the householder in anger said to his servant, Go out quickly to the streets and lanes of the city, and bring in the poor and maimed and blind and lame,' And the servant said, 'Sir, what you commanded has been done, and still there is room. The master said to the servant, 'Go out to the highways and hedges, and compel people to come in, that my house may be filled. For I tell you, none of those men who were invited shall taste my banquet.' 14:25-26 If any one comes to me and does not hate his own father and mother and wife and children and brothers and sisters, yes, and even his own life, he cannot be my disciple.

14:27 Whoever does not bear his own cross and come after me, cannot be my disciple.

14:34-35 Salt is good; but if salt has lost its taste, how shall its saltiness be restored? It is fit neither for the land nor for the dunghill; men throw it away. He who has ears to hear, let him hear.

15:3-7 What man among you, having a hundred sheep, if he has lost one of them, does not leave the ninety-nine in the wilderness, and go after the one which is lost, until he finds it? And when he has found it, he lays it on his shoulders, rejoicing. When he comes home, he calls together his friends and his neighbors, saying to them, 'Rejoice with me, for I have found my sheep which was lost.' Just so, I tell you, there will be more joy in heaven over one sinner who repents than over ninety-nine righteous persons who need no repentance.'

16:13 No servant can serve two masters; for either he will hate the one and love the other, or he will be devoted to the one and despise the other. You cannot serve God and mammon.

16:16 The law and the prophets were until John; since then the good news of the kingdom of God is preached, and every one enters it violently.

16:17 It is easier for heaven and earth to pass away, than for one dot of the law to become void.

16:18 Every one who divorces his wife and marries another commits adultery, and he who marries a woman divorced from her husband commits adultery.

17:1-2 Temptations to sin are sure to come; but woe to him by whom they come! It would be better for him if a millstone were hung round his neck and he were cast into the sea, than that he should cause one of these little ones to sin.

17:3-4 If your brother sins, rebuke him, and if he repents, forgive him; and if he sins against you seven times in the day, and turns to you seven times, and says, 'I repent,' you must forgive him.

17:5-6 The apostles said to the Lord, "Increase our faith!" The Lord said, "If you had faith as a grain of mustard seed, you could say to this mulberry tree, 'Be rooted up, and be planted in the sea,' and it would obey you."

17:23 They will say to you, 'Lo, there!' or 'Lo, here!' Do not go, do not follow them.

17:24 As the lightning lights up the sky from one side to the other, so will Son of man be in his day.

17:26-27 As it was in the days of Noah, so will it be in the days of the Son of man. They ate, they drank, they married, they were given in marriage, until the day when Noah entered the ark, and the flood came and destroyed then all.

17:28-30 As it was in the days of Lot; they ate, they drank, they bought, they sold, they planted, they built, but on the day when Lot went out from Sodom fire and brimstone rained from heaven and destroyed them all. So will it be on the day when the Son of man is revealed.

17:33 Whoever seeks to gain his life will lose it, but whoever loses his life will preserve it.

17:34-35 I tell you, in that night there will be two men in one bed; one will be taken and the other left. There will be two women grinding together; one will be taken and the other left.

17:37 They said to him, "Where Lord?" He said to them, "Where the corpse is, there the eagles will be gathered together."

19:12-24 He said to them, "A nobleman went into a far country to receive kingly power and then return. Calling ten of his servants, he gave them ten pounds, and said to them, 'Trade with these till I come.' But his citizens hated him and sent an embassy after him, saying, 'We do not want this man to reign over us.' When he returned, having received the kingly power, he commanded these servants to whom he had given the money, to be called to him, that he might know what they had gained by trading. The first came before him saying 'Lord, your pound has made ten pounds more.' And he said to him, 'Well done, good servant! Because you have been faithful in a very little, you shall have authority over ten cities.' The second came, saying, 'Lord, your pound has made five pounds,' He said to him; 'And you are to be over five cities.' Then another came, saying, 'Lord here is your pound, which I kept laid away in a napkin; for I was afraid of you, because you are a severe man; you take up what you did not lay down, and reap what you did not sow.' He said to him, 'I will condemn you out of your own mouth, you wicked servant! You knew that I was a severe man, taking up what I did not lay down and reaping what I did not sow? Why then did you not put my money into the bank, and at my coming I should have collected it with interest?' He said to those who stood by, 'Take the pound from him, and give it to him who has ten pounds.' They said to him, 'Lord, he has ten pounds!'

19:25-27 I tell you, that to every one who has more will be given; but from him who has not, even what he has will be taken away.

22:28-30 You are those who have continued with me in my trials; as my Father appointed a kingdom for me, so do I appoint for you that you may eat and drink at my table in my kingdom, and sit on thrones judging the twelve tribes of Israel.

Look for other fine books by Joseph Lumpkin.

The Lost Book Of Enoch: A Comprehensive Transliteration,
ISBN: 0974633666

The Books of Enoch: A Complete Volume Containing 1 Enoch (The Ethiopic Book of Enoch), 2 Enoch (The Slavonic Secrets of Enoch), 3 Enoch (The Hebrew Book of Enoch)
ISBN-13: 978-1933580807

The Encyclopedia of Lost and Rejected Scriptures: The Pseudepigrapha and Apocrypha
ISBN-13: 978-1933580913

The Book of Jubilees; The Little Genesis, The Apocalypse of Moses
ISBN: 193358009

The Book Of Jasher
The J. H. Parry Text in Modern English
ISBN: 1933580143

The Gnostic Gospels of Philip, Mary Magdalene, and Thomas ISBN: 1933580135

The Gospel of Thomas: A Contemporary Translation
ISBN: 0976823349

Fallen Angels, The Watchers, and the Origins of Evil:
A Problem of Choice
ISBN: 1933580100

End of Days: The Apocalyptic Writings
The Apocalypse of Abraham, The Apocalypse of Thomas, or The Revelation of Thomas, 4 Ezra, also referred to as 2 Esdras or the Apocalypse of Ezra, 2 Baruch, also known as the Syriac. Apocalypse of Baruch
ISBN: 1-933580-38-0

www.ingramcontent.com/pod-product-compliance
Lightning Source LLC
Chambersburg PA
CBHW070808100426
42742CB00012B/2292